D0745187

jill dupleix

good cooking
the new basics

photography by Peter Cassidy

Publishing director
Jane O'Shea
Creative director
Mary Evans
Project editors
Janet Illsley
Norma MacMillan
Photographer
Peter Cassidy
Food stylist
Sunil Vijayakar
Props stylist
Roisin Nield
Production
Rebecca Short

NOTES
All eggs are free-range and large; all herbs are fresh; all salt is coarse sea salt, and all pepper is freshly ground black pepper, unless otherwise stated.

First published in 2005 by
Quadrille Publishing Limited

This edition published by
Silverback Books, Inc.,
San Francisco, California.
http://www.silverbackbooks.com
in © 2005

Text © 2005 Jill Dupleix
Photography © 2005 Peter Cassidy
Design and layout © 2005
Quadrille Publishing Limited

The rights of the author have
been asserted.

Cataloguing in Publication Data:
a catalogue record for this book
is available from the British Library.

ISBN 1-59637-017-3

Printed in China

Good cooking is all about making yourself feel good, in the kitchen and at the table. Sure, it's about generosity, hospitality, and the inner glow that comes from feeding friends and family, but let's face it, if you're happy, they're happy. So work out how to use food to make yourself happy.

For me, that means re-writing the rulebook according to strictly modern principles, finding new and better ways with favorite flavors and much-loved classics. I love food, but only when it makes me feel good, not guilty. I love cooking, too, but not when I could be eating and drinking.

The new basics are fresher, lighter, and simpler than the old basics, without the floury sauces, the cream, the pastry, and the deep-frying. Good cooking simply doesn't need them. All it needs is clever staples such as extra virgin olive oil, Parmesan cheese, chili peppers, maple syrup, mustard, sea salt, herbs, and chocolate, and additives—real ones—in the form of ginger, yogurt, fresh lime, anchovies, sesame seeds, and soy sauce. And lots of good ideas that can be used time and again.

Good shopping is 70% of good cooking. Buy great bacon and it won't ooze water in the pan. Buy real sourdough bread and it will be sturdy enough to take whatever you put on it. Buy fresh vegetables in season—preferably from a market stall—and you can cook them in the simplest way possible.

I am also a great believer in fast cooking, because speed captures the goodness in food. Every dish has its prime moment when flavor, color, and nutritional value are at their peak, and the recipes in this book try to capture that moment. Sometimes, though, slow, easy cooking is the answer, if only because the food does all the work and not you. I like that in a recipe.

Good cooking is its own reward. If we shop well and cook well, we eat well and feel well. Spread the joy.

snacks

soups

snacks

soups

grilled tomato soup

A brilliant soup with a lovely smoky flavor. Serve it as a summery first course, or for lunch with country bread.

12 vine-ripened tomatoes
2 tbsp olive oil
2 garlic cloves, smashed
3 cups vegetable or chicken
   stock
1 cup tomato juice or V8
pinch of dried red pepper
   flakes
pinch of sugar
sea salt and pepper
2 tbsp freshly grated Parmesan
1 tbsp oregano leaves
1 tbsp extra virgin olive oil

Heat the broiler. Brush the tomatoes with a little of the olive oil. Place under the broiler and cook until the skin scorches and starts to peel, 15 to 20 minutes. Let cool slightly.

Reserve 4 tomatoes for serving. Peel and roughly chop the rest, saving the juices. Combine the chopped flesh and juices in a saucepan with the remaining olive oil and the garlic, vegetable stock, tomato juice, red pepper flakes, sugar, sea salt, and pepper. Simmer for 15 minutes.

Taste for salt, pepper, and sweetness, and adjust if necessary. Take out the garlic, if you remember.

Place the reserved tomatoes in four warm bowls and ladle the soup over them. Scatter the Parmesan and oregano leaves on top, drizzle with the extra virgin olive oil, and serve.

cocktail nachos

Who would think that lurking in a bag of corn chips are dozens of cute little canapés? If you can't get pickled jalapeños, use any mild, fresh green chili.

MAKES 40

7 oz Cheddar cheese
4 oz pickled green jalapeño peppers
40 salted corn chips
cilantro leaves for serving
CHILI SALSA
1 tbsp olive oil
3 shallots, peeled and finely diced
2 garlic cloves, crushed
1 cup canned crushed tomatoes
2 tbsp chopped cilantro
$1/2$ tsp dried red pepper flakes
1 tsp sugar
$1/2$ tsp sea salt
squeeze of lime juice

To make the chili salsa, heat the olive oil in a pan and cook the shallots until soft. Add the garlic, tomatoes, cilantro, pepper flakes, sugar, and salt, and cook until thick and sludgy, about 20 minutes. Add the lime juice and blend to a smooth sauce using a blender, then let cool.

Heat the oven to 400°F. Shred the cheese, and finely slice the jalapeño peppers. Lay out 40 unbroken corn chips on two baking sheets, and top each one with a little shredded cheese and a slice or two of jalapeño.

Bake until the cheese melts and the corn chips are hot and crisp, 5 to 10 minutes.

Add a tiny dab of chili salsa and a cilantro leaf to each corn chip, and serve hot.

mussels in tomato broth

This is one of those dishes that is an open invitation to slurp, as you dig out mussels and soak up the soupy juices with crackers or crusty bread. If you want a more polite chowder, then remove the mussels from their shells.

SERVES 4

1 lb baking potatoes
1 onion, peeled
1 tbsp butter
4 bacon slices, diced
3 celery stalks, finely diced
1 tsp thyme leaves
3 tbsp chopped parsley, plus
    extra for serving
14-oz can crushed tomatoes
sea salt and pepper
3 lb mussels in shell, rinsed
$^1/_2$ cup white wine

Peel and dice the potatoes. Halve and finely slice the onion. Melt the butter in a large frying pan and cook the bacon, onion, and celery for 10 minutes. Add the potatoes, thyme, parsley, tomatoes, seasoning, and 4 cups water, stirring well. Bring to a boil and simmer for 20 minutes.

Scrub the mussels, discarding any that are broken, and yank out the little beards. Bring the white wine and 1 cup water to a boil in a large pot. Add the mussels, cover tightly, and cook for 2 minutes, then use a slotted spoon to remove the mussels as they open, discarding any with unopened shells.

Strain the mussel broth through a cheesecloth-lined sieve into the soup. Add the mussels to the broth, shelled or unshelled, along with any juices. Gently heat for 5 minutes.

Ladle into warm soup bowls and sprinkle with a little extra chopped parsley. Serve with crackers, for crumbling into the soup as you eat.

sherry clams with jamon

Cured ham and sherry give this clam broth a wonderfully rounded Spanish flavor. Serve it as part of a meal of tapas, with glasses of lightly chilled, fine Jerez (sherry).

SERVES 4

2 oz cured ham or jamon, thickly sliced

1 small onion, peeled

2 tbsp olive oil

$1/4$ cup Spanish sherry

1 tbsp chopped flat-leaf parsley

1 lb small, fresh hardshell clams in shell

Cut the ham into $1/2$-inch squares. Finely slice the onion. Heat the olive oil in a heavy frying pan and cook the onion until soft, about 5 minutes. Add the ham and stir it through. Add the sherry and bring to a boil.

Add the clams and clamp the lid on tightly. Let boil for 2 minutes, then give the pan a big shake. Remove the lid and use a pair of tongs to remove the clams as they open.

When all the clams have opened (throw away any that don't), return them to the pan and toss well in the sauce. Sprinkle with the chopped parsley and serve warm or at room temperature.

extra

pinchos & montaditos
Turn a simple dish into a casual, easy meal of Spanish tapas by adding a few little snackettes, defined as good-things-on-bread that you eat with your fingers.

to make pinchos slice a crusty baguette on the diagonal, and lightly toast. Top with folds of roasted red bell pepper and sliced jamon (cured ham); smoky piquillo peppers with olives and anchovies; manchego cheese and membrillo quince paste; sizzled smoked chorizo sausage and white bean purée; seared shrimp with aïoli; smoked salmon and piquillo peppers; sliced tomatoes and anchovies.

serve with lots of chilled sherry or cold beers.

arugula cocktail

This is an amazing way to crank-start the appetite—dramatic and elegant, with a chlorophyllic, peppery, lemony flavor that is missing from your normal everyday cocktails. I discovered it at Heinz Beck's food-forward La Pergola restaurant at the Rome Cavalieri Hilton, and fell instantly in love with it.

SERVES 6

4 oz arugula leaves
2 cups ginger ale
8 oz lemon sorbet

In a blender, work the arugula, ginger ale, and lemon sorbet at high speed until you have a smooth green liquid. Pour into chilled large martini glasses and serve.

You can make the cocktail beforehand, but it should always be icy cold, and should always be re-blended for a few seconds before serving. Think of it as a chilled arugula gazpacho, and slip in a dash of frozen vodka, if you like.

chive brot

I came across this wild-tasting, chive-carpeted rye bread in Vienna, and again in Munich, and co-opted it for my favorite *smorrebrod* meal of salmon, boiled egg, and salmon roe. To serve with drinks, make it in miniature with quail eggs.

SERVES 4

1 large egg
2 oz chives, plus extra for
 serving
4 thin, square slices
 pumpernickel or rye bread
4 tbsp cream cheese or
 unsalted butter
14 oz smoked or cured
 salmon, finely sliced
2 oz salmon roe
freshly ground black pepper
1 lemon, quartered

Add the egg to a small pan of hot water and bring to a boil. Simmer for 8 minutes, then drain and cool under cold running water.

With a pair of scissors, finely snip the chives (and I mean *finely* snip) and arrange on a flat plate.

Spread the rye bread with the cream cheese or butter, right to the edges. Lay the bread spread-side down on the chives, pressing lightly, to cover each slice with a fine layer of chives, from edge to edge.

Peel and finely slice the egg, using an egg-slicer. Lay the chive bread on a plate. Top each with a fold of salmon, an egg slice, and a teaspoonful of salmon roe, and grind some black pepper over. Add a whole chive and serve with a wedge of lemon.

miang kum

These little Thai, leaf-wrapped appetizers pack a mean punch of hot, sour, sweet, and smoky flavors. Cha plu leaves are available from Thai markets. Replace the salmon with shredded, cooked chicken, pork, or shrimp, if you like.

MAKES 12

12 cha plu, spinach, or
   lettuce leaves
7 oz hot-smoked salmon fillet
2 kaffir lime leaves
1 tbsp finely diced lime
2 tbsp peanuts, chopped
1 tbsp chopped cilantro
2 oz salmon roe

HOT-SOUR-SWEET SAUCE
2 shallots, finely sliced
1 garlic clove, crushed
$\frac{1}{2}$ small, hot red chili pepper
2 tbsp peanuts
$\frac{1}{2}$ cup brown sugar
1 tbsp fish sauce
1 tbsp tamarind concentrate

To make the sauce, pound the shallots in a mortar with the garlic, diced chili, and peanuts to a paste. In a saucepan, mix this paste with the sugar, fish sauce, tamarind, and 1 tbsp water, and bring to a boil, stirring. Simmer, stirring, until thick and syrupy, about 5 minutes. Let cool.

Wash and dry the leaves and set out on a tray. Shred the smoked salmon into bite-sized pieces, discarding any bones and skin.

Fold each kaffir lime leaf in half along the spine, then cut away and discard the spine. Cut the leaves lengthwise into extremely thin strips and set aside.

Top each whole leaf with some smoked salmon and a teaspoonful of sauce. (If the sauce is too firm, beat in a spoonful of boiling water.) Scatter diced lime, peanuts, and cilantro over. Top with a little salmon roe and shredded kaffir lime leaf, wrap, and eat.

red pepper hot cakes

I grew up on fritters made with leftover roast lamb, and have loved the genre ever since. Make these with cooked chicken, duck, or pork instead of ham, or with leftover potatoes and peas.

SERVES 4

1 large red bell pepper
1 thick slice ham, diced
2 tbsp freshly grated Parmesan
2 tbsp chopped parsley
sea salt and pepper
1 tbsp vegetable oil
BATTER
3/4 cup all-purpose flour
1 tsp baking powder
large pinch of cayenne pepper
2 eggs, separated
2/3 cup milk

To make the batter, sift the flour, baking powder, and cayenne into a bowl. Add the egg yolks and lightly mix, then slowly add the milk, beating with a wooden spoon until smooth. Beat the egg whites in another bowl until peaky, and fold into the batter.

Finely dice the pepper, discarding the core and seeds. Add to the batter with the ham, Parmesan, parsley, sea salt, and pepper, mixing lightly.

Heat half the oil in a nonstick frying pan. When hot, drop 4 tablespoons of the batter into the pan, keeping them separate. Turn the heat to low. When holes appear on top of the batter, turn and cook the other side until golden, 3 to 4 minutes longer. Remove and keep warm.

Heat the remaining oil in the pan and make another 4 fritters. Serve for brunch, lunch, or supper, with an avocado salad.

sweet potato & bean soup

This simple soup would be quite nice on its own—but add a little curry powder and your spoon just can't leave it alone. Serve it in small bowls as a first course, or with warm Indian bread for a family supper.

2$^1/_4$ lb orange-fleshed sweet
   potatoes
5 cups boiling water or
   vegetable stock
sea salt and pepper
14-oz can white beans, such
   as cannellini, drained and
   rinsed
1 tsp good curry powder,
   or more to taste
$^1/_3$ cup plain low-fat yogurt
pinch of paprika
2 tbsp cilantro or parsley
   leaves

Peel the sweet potatoes, cut into small cubes, and put into a pan. Add the boiling water or stock, sea salt, and pepper, and bring to a boil. Simmer until the sweet potato is soft, about 15 minutes.

Add half the beans and the curry powder, stirring well, then purée in a food processor in batches, being careful not to overfill the bowl.

Return to the pan, add the remaining whole beans, and heat gently. If too thick, add extra boiling water. Taste for salt, pepper, and curry powder.

Ladle the soup into warm bowls. Swirl a generous dollop of yogurt into each bowl and sprinkle with a little paprika. Scatter the cilantro or parsley leaves on top and serve.

veggies
salads
veggies
salads

summer vegetable carpaccio

The new carpaccio is of vegetables, not beef—finely sliced, crisp summer vegetables dressed with a lemony vinaigrette. If you grow small, tender carrots or green beans, or have edible flowers, such as chive flowers, add them too.

SERVES 4

2 celery stalks
8 small pink radishes
10 fava bean pods
small wedge of Parmesan for shaving
1 fennel bulb
1 tbsp salted capers, rinsed

DRESSING
2 tbsp extra virgin olive oil
1 tbsp lemon juice
sea salt and pepper

Finely slice the celery on an extreme diagonal. Finely slice the radishes. Shell the fava beans, and cook in simmering water until tender, about 5 minutes. Cool under running water, then peel off the outer skins.

Using a vegetable peeler, carefully shave thin slices of Parmesan onto a sheet of paper or foil. To make the dressing, whisk the olive oil, lemon juice, and seasoning together in a bowl.

At the last minute, trim off the stems and any tough outer leaves from the fennel, then slice across the bulb as finely as possible. Drop the sliced fennel into the dressing and toss well.

Scatter the fennel lightly over four dinner plates. Toss the celery, radishes, and fava beans in the remaining dressing and scatter on top, as if you are topping a pizza. Drizzle with any remaining dressing, and finish with the capers and Parmesan shavings.

avocado & grapefruit salad

Rich, creamy avocado is cut back by the citrus sharpness of grapefruit in this Israeli-inspired salad. It's brilliant for a brunchy breakfast, and teams well with grilled salmon, tuna, or mackerel for dinner.

SERVES 4

1 ripe grapefruit
2 tbsp extra virgin olive oil
 or walnut oil
sea salt and pepper
2 large, ripe avocados
2 heads baby romaine
3 tbsp roughly chopped
 cilantro leaves
pinch of pink peppercorns,
 crushed

Hold the grapefruit over a bowl to catch the juices, and peel it thickly, removing all white pith. Cut the grapefruit between the membrane into sections. Whisk the juices with the olive or walnut oil, sea salt, and pepper to make the dressing.

Cut each avocado in half lengthwise, remove the pit, and peel off the skin. Cut the flesh into long, thin slices and carefully toss in the dressing along with the grapefruit sections.

Separate the lettuce leaves, wash, and pat dry, then tear into bite-sized pieces. Lightly toss the avocado and grapefruit with the leaves and half the cilantro, then drain off any excess dressing.

Serve in cute cocktail glasses or on a large platter. Scatter the crushed pink peppercorns and the remaining cilantro on top.

asian herb salad

This has a wonderfully wild freshness about it, which is achieved by massive overuse of delicate herbs and my all-time favorite sweet-and-sour vinaigrette.

SERVES 4

4 oz arugula leaves
4 oz mint
4 oz basil
4 oz cilantro
1 oz chervil
2/3 cup canned bamboo shoots

DRESSING

2 shallots, peeled, halved,
  and finely sliced
1 tbsp rice vinegar
1 tsp sugar
2 tbsp extra virgin olive oil
1 tsp toasted sesame oil
1 tbsp mirin
sea salt and pepper

For the dressing, mix the shallots, rice vinegar, and sugar together in a small bowl and set aside.

Trim any excess stems from the arugula, and pick the herb leaves from their stems. Rinse and spin dry the arugula and herbs. Cut the bamboo shoots into matchsticks.

To make the dressing, whisk the olive oil, sesame oil, mirin, sea salt, and pepper together in a large bowl. Stir in the shallot mixture, then taste and adjust the flavors.

Very lightly toss the arugula, bamboo shoots, and herbs in the dressing, and serve, with chopsticks.

rumbledethumps

It's cold. You're feeling blue. You need rumbledethumps, an irresistibly comforting dish from the Scottish Borders in which potatoes are mashed with cabbage and topped with melting cheese. If you're feeling really depressed, top with a fried egg.

SERVES 4

1 lb all-purpose potatoes
14 oz Savoy cabbage
sea salt and pepper
6 green onions, minced
2 tbsp butter
$1/4$ cup shredded Cheddar
    cheese
$1/4$ cup freshly grated
    Parmesan

Heat the oven to 350°F. Peel the potatoes and cut into rough chunks. Remove any tough outer leaves and the core from the cabbage, and finely slice the leaves.

Cook the potatoes in a large pan of simmering, salted water for 10 minutes, then add the cabbage and cook until both are tender, but not overly soft, about 10 minutes longer. Add the green onions for the last minute of cooking. Drain well.

Add the butter and most of the cheeses, and mash together well, seasoning with salt and pepper.

You can serve the rumbledethumps at this stage, sprinkled with the rest of the cheese. Or, dump it into a buttered baking dish, sprinkle with the cheese, and bake until lightly browned and steaming hot, 25 to 30 minutes.

fruit & vegetable tagine

This rich, fruity, spicy, aromatic tagine brings vegetables to life. Serve with steamy golden couscous, Morocco's national dish.

SERVES 4

1 large onion, peeled

2 tbsp olive oil

2 garlic cloves, crushed

1 tsp ground coriander

$1/2$ tsp ground ginger

$1/2$ tsp saffron powder

14 oz sweet potato, peeled

8 baby carrots, peeled

14-oz can crushed tomatoes

$1^3/_4$ cups vegetable stock

8 green olives, cracked

8 dried apricots or figs

1 tsp harissa or chili sauce

1 tbsp clear honey

2 cinnamon sticks

14 oz zucchini

8 plump Medjool dates

Halve and finely slice the onion. Heat the olive oil in a heavy pan and gently cook the onion for 10 minutes, stirring well. Add the garlic, coriander, ginger, and saffron, stirring well.

Roughly chop the sweet potato and add to the pan along with the carrots, tomatoes, stock, olives, apricots or figs, harissa or chili sauce, honey, sea salt, pepper, and cinnamon sticks, stirring. Cover the pan and simmer for 15 minutes.

Roughly chop the zucchini and add to the pan along with the dates. Simmer until the vegetables are tender but not falling apart, about 15 minutes longer. Taste for salt and pepper, and serve hot.

extra

easy couscous Combine 1½ cups quick cooking couscous, 2 tbsp extra virgin olive oil, salt, and pepper in a bowl. Add 2 cups boiling water, cover, and leave for 10 minutes. Fluff up with a fork. Keep warm over simmering water until ready to serve.

green couscous Add 2 tbsp each lemon juice and minced cilantro and parsley with the water.

red couscous Add a 14-oz can of tomatoes, drained and chopped, 2 cinnamon sticks, and 1 tsp ground cumin with the water.

lemon couscous Add 2 tbsp diced preserved lemon, 1 tsp dried mint, 2 tbsp minced mint, and 1 tbsp toasted sliced almonds with the water.

moroccan café salad

Here's a hearty, warm salad of roasted vegetables tossed with a fruity, saffron dressing and served with feathery leaves of frisée and the crunch of pine nuts.

SERVES 4

2 zucchini
2 eggplants
2 parsnips, peeled
2 tbsp olive oil
1 tbsp thyme sprigs
sea salt and pepper
8 oz cherry tomatoes
1 head of frisée
1 tbsp pine nuts, toasted

DRESSING

large pinch of saffron threads
  (about 20)
1 tbsp raisins
2 tbsp extra virgin olive oil
1 tbsp red wine vinegar
1 tsp Dijon mustard

Heat the oven to 400°F. For the dressing, put the saffron and raisins in 2 tbsp boiling water and set aside to soak.

Trim the zucchini, eggplants, and parsnips, and quarter lengthwise. Toss in the olive oil along with the thyme, sea salt, and pepper, then tip into a roasting pan. Roast for 30 minutes.

Toss the vegetables, then add the cherry tomatoes and roast until the vegetables are scorched and soft, about 10 minutes longer. Let cool for 10 minutes.

To make the dressing, whisk the olive oil, wine vinegar, mustard, sea salt, and pepper in a large bowl with the saffron, raisins, and soaking water.

Trim the frisée and tear the leaves in half. Toss the leaves in half the dressing and arrange in serving bowls. Toss the warm vegetables and cherry tomatoes in the remaining dressing and strew over the top. Scatter the toasted pine nuts over each salad and serve.

soy sauce

Soy sauce adds instant complexity with its mysterious fermented soybean flavor. Keep a bottle handy, and don't just use it for the stir-fry. Add a dash of soy to soups, stews, and roasts for another layer of flavor.

which soy? Dark soy is black and strong; light soy is dark brown and salty; tamari is wheat-free; and Japanese soy is light, elegant, and all-purpose (e.g. Kikkoman, Yamasa).

spice up your soy Add 4 star anise, 3 dried hot chili peppers, and 20 peppercorns to $1\frac{1}{4}$ cups soy sauce. Leave in a lidded jar for a week. Use for marinades, dips, and noodles.

lemon-soy dip Mix 3 tbsp soy sauce with 1 tbsp lemon juice. Cut sashimi-quality tuna into bite-sized cubes and dip into the lemon-soy. Serve with wasabi paste.

sweet soy omelet Beat 2 eggs with 1 tsp soy, 1 tsp mirin, sea salt, and pepper. Heat 1 tsp oil in a wok, swirling to coat the surface. Add the egg and swirl again. Cook briefly until set, then loosen the edges and unmold. Roll up and thinly slice. Add to stir-fries, noodles, and rice.

honey-roast carrots Scrub and trim two bunches of baby carrots. Coat them in 2 tbsp soy, 2 tbsp olive oil, 1 tsp honey, sea salt, and pepper. Roast at 400°F until browned and tender, about 20 minutes.

steamed soy fish Mix 2 tbsp soy with 1 tsp toasted sesame oil and 1 tbsp Chinese rice wine. Pour onto two 6-oz white fish fillets on a heatproof platter. Scatter shredded ginger, chili, and cilantro on the fish. Steam until cooked, about 10 minutes. Serve with rice or noodles.

double happiness beans

Fermented black beans, which are soybeans preserved in salt, are available from Chinese food stores. I made up the bit about double happiness, but the combination of the two beans certainly does it for me.

SERVES 4

2 tbsp fermented black beans
3/4-inch piece of ginger, peeled
10 oz fine green beans
1 red bell pepper
sea salt
2 tbsp vegetable oil
1 garlic clove, smashed
1/2 small, hot red chili pepper, finely sliced
1 tbsp Chinese rice wine or dry sherry
2 tbsp soy sauce
1 tsp toasted sesame oil
1 tsp cornstarch mixed with 1 tbsp cold water

Soak the black beans in cold water for 10 minutes, then drain. Cut the ginger into thin matchsticks. Trim the green beans. Cut the red pepper into thin strips, discarding the core and seeds.

Cook the green beans and red pepper in a pan of simmering, salted water for 3 minutes, then drain and refresh under cold running water. Drain again, and pat dry with a clean dish towel.

Heat the oil in a wok or frying pan, then add the garlic, ginger, and chili, tossing well. Add the green beans and red pepper, and toss well for 2 minutes over a high heat. Add the black beans, rice wine, soy sauce, and sesame oil, and toss well for 1 minute longer.

Add the cornstarch mixture and toss over the heat until the sauce thickens and coats the vegetables. Serve hot, with steamed rice.

airport potatoes

I pinched this from the warming trays of the cafeteria at Rome Airport, long a source of wonderful ideas. I often serve it with grilled fish or chicken, but you could make a meal of it.

SERVES 4

2^1/$_4$ lb all-purpose potatoes, peeled
1 tbsp olive oil for pan
sea salt and pepper
14-oz can crushed tomatoes
2 tbsp extra virgin olive oil
2 garlic cloves, crushed
^{1}/$_2$ tsp dried oregano
1 tbsp salted capers, rinsed
2 tbsp roughly chopped parsley
8 oz cherry tomatoes

Heat the oven to 375°F. Finely slice the potatoes and roughly layer in an oiled roasting pan. Add 1 cup water and season with salt and pepper. Cover the pan with foil and bake for 30 minutes.

Combine the canned tomatoes with the extra virgin olive oil, garlic, oregano, capers, half the chopped parsley, and sea salt and pepper.

Remove the foil, and pour the tomato mixture over the potatoes. Cut the cherry tomatoes in half and scatter on top. Continue baking until the potatoes are tender and starting to crisp at the edges, about 30 minutes longer. Sprinkle with the remaining chopped parsley and serve.

zucchini with mint & almonds

This speedy dish has an Italian accent. It really belongs to New York chef Jimmy Bradley of The Red Cat, who cuts the zucchini very, very finely and tosses them over a superhigh heat for just a few seconds.

SERVES 4

1 lb zucchini
2 tbsp olive oil
$^1/_4$ cup sliced almonds
1 tbsp mint leaves, torn if large
sea salt and pepper

Cut off the ends of the zucchini, then cut across into three short sections. Slice each section lengthwise, then cut each slice into matchsticks.

Heat the olive oil in a frying pan over medium heat, add the sliced almonds, and toast until golden.

Add the zucchini to the hot pan, and toss over high heat until just cooked, 1 to 2 minutes. Don't overcook until limp.

Scatter the mint leaves, sea salt, and pepper over the top, and serve on four warm plates as a first course, or one large platter as a side dish.

grains

greens

grains

greens

goat cheese, beans & walnuts

Compatible flavors are often natural companions. Whenever I eat this, I always imagine goats grazing contentedly under walnut trees, their milk transformed into fresh tangy cheese. This magical place may not actually exist, but it should.

SERVES 4

10 oz fresh goat cheese
    (in log form)
1¼ lb fine green beans
1 cup walnut halves
sea salt and pepper

MARINADE

7 tbsp extra virgin olive oil
1 tbsp walnut oil
2 shallots, peeled and finely
    sliced
1 garlic clove, flattened
1 tsp thyme leaves
1 tsp coriander seeds, cracked
1 tsp fennel seeds

To marinate the goat cheese, cut it into thick slices and arrange in a single layer on a platter. Combine the olive and walnut oils, shallots, garlic, thyme, and coriander and fennel seeds, then pour this over the cheese. Cover with plastic wrap, and leave until serving.

Trim the green beans. Cook in simmering, salted water until tender, about 5 minutes, then drain. Toast the walnut halves in a hot dry pan until fragrant.

Heat the broiler. Drain off a little marinade from the cheese and toss the beans in it, adding sea salt and pepper. Arrange the beans on large serving plates.

Gently lift the cheese slices onto a sheet of foil and put under the broiler until just melted. Place on the beans. Spoon the remaining marinade over and scatter the toasted walnuts on top, then serve.

abruzzese lentil soup

You could virtually live on this rustic, slow-cooked soup. Lentils are low in fat, high in protein, and easy to cook, and they taste delicious. Look for the small lentils from Umbria or Abruzzo in Italy, or from Puy in France, which hold their shape well and taste deliciously nutty.

SERVES 6

$1^1/_4$ cups small brown or
   green lentils
2 garlic cloves, smashed
2 bay leaves
1 onion, peeled and halved
2 celery stalks
2 carrots, peeled
2 tbsp olive oil
14-oz can crushed tomatoes
14-oz can chickpeas, drained
sea salt and pepper
2 tbsp chopped parsley
freshly grated Parmesan for
   serving

Rinse the lentils, then place in a pan with the garlic, bay leaves, and 6 cups cold water. Cook until almost tender, about 30 minutes, skimming occasionally.

In the meantime, finely slice the onion and celery, and dice the carrots. Heat the olive oil in a large saucepan. Add the onion, carrots, and celery, and cook, stirring often, for 10 minutes.

Add the tomatoes and stir well, then add the lentils and their cooking water. Simmer until nice and soupy, about 20 minutes.

Add the chickpeas, sea salt, and pepper, and simmer for at least 10 minutes or longer, adding extra water as necessary.

Stir in the chopped parsley and ladle into warm soup bowls. Serve with grated Parmesan.

bulghur shrimp salad

Juicy, crunchy bulghur—or burghul or bulgur (that grainy stuff in tabbouleh)—is the perfect foil for shrimp, avocado, and preserved lemon, in one of the freshest salads around. Drizzle with parsley oil for even more fresh flavor.

SERVES 4

1¹/₄ cups fine bulghur wheat

12 raw large shrimp in shells

sea salt and pepper

3 tbsp extra virgin olive oil,
  plus extra for serving

2 tbsp lemon juice, plus extra
  for serving

1 avocado

2 tbsp roughly chopped
  cilantro

2 tbsp chopped preserved
  lemon

Put the bulghur into a large heatproof bowl and pour on 1³/₄ cups boiling water. Stir, then let stand for 30 minutes.

Cook the shrimp lightly in a pan of simmering, salted water, until just pink and no longer transparent. Remove and let cool.

In a large bowl, whisk the olive oil and lemon juice with sea salt and pepper. Cut the avocado in half, remove the pit, peel, and chop. Add the chopped avocado, cilantro, and preserved lemon to the dressing.

Drain the bulghur of any unabsorbed water, then squeeze dry and toss with the dressing.

Peel the shrimp, leaving the tails. Toss in a little extra olive oil and lemon juice, and arrange on top of the bulghur salad.

extra

parsley or basil oil

Use to add brilliant color, flavor, and fragrance to salads, soups, fish, and— best of all—roast chicken.

to prepare plunge 3 oz flat-leaf parsley or basil into a pan of fast boiling water for 15 seconds. Remove and immediately plunge into a bowl of cold water filled with ice cubes. Drain and squeeze dry. Roughly chop and blend with 5 tbsp olive oil for 10 seconds. Add 5 tbsp vegetable oil and blend for 1 minute. Let drain through dampened cheesecloth, or a sieve lined with a paper coffee filter, for several hours.

store in a lidded jar in the fridge and use within 1 week, or freeze in ice cube trays for future use.

summer rice with basil

Think of this as a hot rice salad, a summery pilaf that makes a wonderful change from the daily salad—especially if it involves everybody's favorite summer staples: tomato, basil, and zucchini.

SERVES 4

3 shallots, peeled
1 celery stalk
1 tbsp butter
1 tbsp olive oil
1$^{1}/_{4}$ cups arborio rice
$^{1}/_{2}$ cup white wine
5 cups hot chicken or
   vegetable stock
2 large, ripe tomatoes
2 zucchini
1 tbsp extra virgin olive oil
sea salt and pepper
2 tbsp basil leaves
freshly grated Parmesan for
   serving

Finely slice the shallots and celery. Melt the butter with the olive oil in a heavy pan and cook the shallots and celery, stirring, until softened. Add the rice and stir until well coated. Add the wine and let it bubble for a minute or two, stirring, until absorbed.

Add all but one ladleful of stock, stir well, and bring to a boil. Reduce the heat to very low, cover tightly, and cook gently for 18 to 20 minutes, when the surface of the rice should be pock-marked with small holes.

Meanwhile, cut the tomatoes in half, squeeze out the seeds, and cut the flesh into small dice; set aside. Trim and dice the zucchini.

Add the remaining stock and the zucchini to the rice and cook, stirring, for 5 minutes.

Stir in the tomatoes, extra virgin olive oil, and sea salt and pepper to taste. Scatter the basil leaves over and serve with grated Parmesan.

greek bean stew with feta

The traditional beans to use are dried gigantes, which need overnight soaking and long, slow cooking, but for this "I-don't have-all-day" version use canned jumbo lima, cannellini, or red kidney beans instead.

SERVES 4

1 onion, peeled
2 tbsp olive oil, plus extra
  for serving
2 garlic cloves, crushed
14-oz can crushed tomatoes
1 tbsp tomato paste
2 bay leaves
2 tbsp minced parsley
2 tbsp minced dill
1 tsp sea salt
1/2 tsp pepper
1/2 tsp paprika
1 tbsp sugar
3 cups canned beans
4 oz feta cheese

Halve and finely slice the onion. Heat the olive oil in a heavy pan and fry the onion until soft but not browned. Add the garlic, tomatoes, tomato paste, and 2 cups water. Stir in the bay leaves, parsley, half the dill, the sea salt, pepper, paprika, and sugar, and bring to a simmer.

Simmer, partially covered, until nice and thick, 20 to 30 minutes. Drain and rinse the beans, then add them to the stew and simmer gently for 10 minutes longer.

Rinse the feta cheese, pat dry, and cut into chunky cubes. Add to the pan and simmer until the cheese is soft, about 5 minutes.

Serve in small bowls, drizzled with a little extra olive oil and sprinkled with the remaining dill. Serve hot or at room temperature, with some warm flat bread and a Greek salad.

sausage & parsnip risotto

Risotto is one of my favorite cold-weather dishes, the culinary equivalent of a blazing fire and cashmere cushions.

SERVES 4

2 parsnips
sea salt and pepper
1 onion, peeled
2 tbsp butter
1 tbsp olive oil
2 fresh Italian pork sausages
4 rosemary sprigs
1^{1}/$_2$ cups arborio rice
^{2}/$_3$ cup light red wine
5 cups hot chicken stock
1 tbsp tomato paste
1 tbsp minced flat-leaf
  parsley
1 tbsp freshly grated Parmesan

Peel the parsnips, slice thickly, and cook in simmering, salted water for 10 minutes. Drain and set aside.

Halve and finely slice the onion. Melt half of the butter with the olive oil in a heavy pan, add the onion, and cook for a few minutes until softened. Skin the sausages and pinch small portions into the pan. Fry until well browned, then take out half the sausage and set aside.

Add the rosemary and rice to the pan and stir until well coated. Add the wine and let bubble for 2 minutes, stirring, until absorbed.

Add a ladleful of stock to the rice and stir until it is absorbed. Add another ladleful and stir constantly, but calmly, with a wooden spoon until absorbed. Continue this process until the rice is cooked and still creamy, 15 to 20 minutes.

Add the tomato paste, sliced parsnips, reserved sausage, remaining butter, sea salt, pepper, parsley, and Parmesan. Heat through and serve.

sesame

Sesame seeds—black or white—add fresh, nutty flavor to breads, cakes, and salads. Then there is fragrant, toasty sesame oil and nutty, creamy sesame paste (tahini), a brilliant stand-by for instant dips and sauces.

toast sesame seeds in a hot, dry pan for a few seconds before using, for extra flavor.

honey sesame peaches Peel 4 fresh peaches—dip in boiling water for 5 seconds, then peel off the skin. Cut in half and remove pits. Drizzle with a little honey, sprinkle with sesame seeds, and place under a hot broiler until golden, about 3 minutes.

sesame asparagus Lightly toss cooked asparagus in 1 tsp toasted sesame oil. Sprinkle with sesame seeds and serve.

sesame shrimp Take 8 raw jumbo shrimp, remove heads, and snip off legs. Cut in half lengthwise, keeping the shell intact, then flatten. Brush with toasted sesame oil, sprinkle with salt and 1 tbsp sesame seeds, and scorch under a hot broiler for 3 minutes.

dip into dukkah In a hot dry pan, toast $2/3$ cup white sesame seeds, $3/4$ cup blanched almonds, $1/2$ cup coriander seeds, and $1 1/2$ tbsp cumin seeds until fragrant, stirring. Cool, then coarsely grind with 1 tsp sea salt. Dip warm bread first into olive oil, then into dukkah—divine.

tahini tomatoes In a blender, work 2 crushed garlic cloves with 1 tsp sea salt, 2 tbsp lemon juice, 3 tbsp tahini paste, $1/2$ tsp ground cumin, and 2 tbsp water. Add a little extra water until creamy. Drizzle this over sliced tomatoes and scatter some mint on top.

green onion tofu

Fresh or packaged beancurd (dofu in Cantonese, tofu in Japanese) is one of my favorite cool, no-cook dishes, because it so readily absorbs other flavors and looks so fresh with the wild, bright colors of green onions and chili.

SERVES 4

10 oz silken Japanese tofu
4 green onions (green
 part only)
1 large, hot red chili pepper
1 tbsp toasted sesame oil
1 tbsp soy sauce
2 tbsp cilantro leaves

Gently remove the tofu from its packaging, and drain.

Cut the green onion stems into 2-inch lengths. Using the tip of a sharp knife, shred them lengthwise into fine strips.

Trim the chili top and bottom, cut in half, and remove the seeds, then shred lengthwise.

Cut the tofu into four equal blocks and arrange on a serving platter. Drizzle with sesame oil and soy. Toss the green onions, chili, and cilantro together and scatter on top.

Serve one each as a little appetizer, or serve as part of a Japanese or Chinese meal.

spinach & cheese quesadilla

Instant snack or excellent party food, quesadillas are fun to make, especially with wham-bam-pow gorgonzola melting inside.

SERVES 4

1 lb spinach leaves
sea salt and pepper
14 oz fresh mozzarella balls
  (preferably buffalo), drained
7 oz creamy blue cheese
  (e.g. gorgonzola)
8 wheat flour tortillas

Wash the spinach well and cook very briefly in a covered pan, without extra water, until wilted. Drain well, squeeze dry, and finely chop. Add sea salt and pepper, and toss lightly.

Slice the mozzarella finely, and roughly crumble the blue cheese. Arrange some mozzarella slices over a flour tortilla, scatter some blue cheese on top, and strew with spinach. Top with a second flour tortilla.

Transfer to a dry, nonstick frying pan and cook over a medium heat until lightly browned, about 3 minutes. Turn over and cook the other side until it is lightly browned and the cheese has melted.

Transfer to a board and keep warm, while you repeat with the remaining ingredients. Cut in half or into fourths and serve.

noodles

pasta

noodles

pasta

beef rice noodles

If you live near a Chinese food store, look for fresh rice noodles, which have an incomparable slippery, soft texture. To use, pour boiling water over 1 lb noodles, then drain and rinse under cold water before cooking.

SERVES 4

12 oz ribeye or sirloin steak
2 tsp cornstarch
1 tsp toasted sesame oil
1 tbsp Chinese rice wine
4 tbsp soy sauce
7 oz dried rice noodles
3 tbsp vegetable oil, plus
   extra for tossing noodles
1 red bell pepper
4 green onions
2 garlic cloves, finely sliced
3/4-inch piece of ginger, peeled
   and shredded
1 tbsp oyster sauce
1 tsp sugar
2 cups bean sprouts, rinsed

Thinly slice the steak. Mix the cornstarch with the sesame oil, then stir in the rice wine and 1 tbsp soy sauce. Toss the steak in this mixture and let marinate for 30 minutes.

Add the dried noodles to a pan of boiling water and bring back to a boil, stirring. Cover and leave off the heat for 3 minutes, then drain and rinse under cold water. Toss in a little vegetable oil to prevent sticking.

Finely slice the pepper, discarding core and seeds. Slice the green onions on the diagonal. Heat 2 tbsp oil in a wok and add the garlic, ginger, red pepper, and most of the onions. Toss over high heat for 1 minute. Add the beef with its marinade and toss until colored. Tip onto a warm plate.

Heat 1 tbsp oil in the wok, add the noodles, and cook for 2 minutes over high heat. Add the remaining 3 tbsp soy sauce, 2 tbsp water, the oyster sauce, sugar, and bean sprouts, tossing well, then add the beef mixture and combine. Scatter in the remaining green onions and serve.

zucchini carbonara

The principle is the same as for *pasta alla carbonara*, but with zucchini instead of bacon: the heat of the freshly drained pasta cooks the eggs and cheese into a creamy, golden sauce.

SERVES 2

7 oz penne or fine tagliatelle
sea salt and coarsely ground
   black pepper
2 zucchini, about 8 oz
3 egg yolks
6^1/$_2$ tbsp freshly grated
   Parmesan, plus extra for
   serving
1 tsp grated lemon zest

Cook the pasta in plenty of boiling, salted water for 6 minutes. Meanwhile, trim the zucchini and cut lengthwise into thick slices, then into strips, and then into small dice.

Add the zucchini to the pasta pot and cook until they are tender but not overly soft, and the pasta is *al dente*—tender but firm to the bite, about 2 minutes longer.

In a large bowl, beat the egg yolks, Parmesan, lemon zest, sea salt, and pepper together.

Drain the pasta and zucchini, reserving a few spoonfuls of the cooking water. Immediately add to the egg mixture, tossing quickly until the pasta is well coated. Add the reserved hot pasta water if dry, and toss again until lightly creamy.

Sprinkle with extra pepper and Parmesan and serve in warm shallow bowls.

extra

no-cook pasta sauces
3 great recipes to serve 4:

ricotta & prosciutto
Mix 1/2 cup ricotta cheese, 2 tbsp grated Parmesan, 2 tbsp snipped chives, and 4 torn prosciutto slices.

tomato & basil
Mix 4 peeled, seeded, and diced ripe tomatoes with 3 tbsp torn basil leaves, 3 tbsp extra virgin olive oil, 1 crushed garlic clove, sea salt, and pepper.

lemon & parmesan
Mix 1 tbsp grated lemon zest with 2 tbsp grated Parmesan, 2 tbsp roughly chopped parsley, 1 tbsp rinsed capers, and 3 tbsp extra virgin olive oil.

to serve cook 14 oz pasta until *al dente*. Drain, and toss while still very hot with your sauce.

bucatini with sardines

One of the tricks of good cooking is to use what is available and not to fuss too much about what isn't. Have confidence in your ability to turn a few standbys—canned sardines, pasta, capers, tomato purée, and pine nuts—into something delicious, without compromising your own exquisite taste.

SERVES 4

14 oz bucatini (fat spaghetti)
sea salt
1 tbsp olive oil
1 garlic clove, smashed
1 tbsp salted capers, rinsed
1/2 tsp dried red pepper flakes
  or cayenne
2 anchovy fillets, chopped
1 1/4 cups tomato purée or
  14-oz can tomatoes, drained
  and chopped
10-oz can sardines or tuna,
  drained
1 tbsp pine nuts, toasted
1 tbsp roughly torn parsley

Cook the pasta in a large pot of simmering, salted water until *al dente*—tender but firm to the bite.

Meanwhile, heat the olive oil in a large frying pan over a low heat, and add the garlic, capers, pepper flakes or cayenne, and anchovy fillets, stirring. Add the tomato purée or canned tomatoes, stirring well, and simmer for 5 minutes.

When the pasta is almost ready, drain the sardines and roughly chop. Add to the sauce and gently heat through. Drain the pasta, reserving a few spoonfuls of the water, and add the pasta to the sauce, tossing well. If dry, add the reserved hot pasta water.

Scatter the toasted pine nuts and torn parsley over, and serve in warm pasta bowls.

angelhair with crab & lemon

This rich, but light pasta is also lovely made with shrimp. Fast cooking keeps the flavors fresh and light, so that even the tomato is still fresh tomato rather than tomato sauce.

SERVES 4

2 ripe tomatoes
10 oz angelhair or tagliolini
  pasta
sea salt and pepper
2 tbsp extra virgin olive oil,
  plus extra for serving
1 garlic clove, crushed
pinch of dried red pepper flakes
1 tbsp salted capers, rinsed
3 tbsp dry white wine
2$^{1}/_{2}$ cups cooked crabmeat
1 tbsp lemon juice
2 tbsp chopped parsley
1 tbsp chopped basil
2 tsp finely grated lemon zest

Cut the tomatoes in half and squeeze out and discard the seeds and juice. Finely chop the flesh and set aside.

Cook the pasta in a large pan of boiling, salted water until *al dente*— tender but firm to the bite. (Angelhair will cook in just 2 minutes.)

Heat the olive oil in a frying pan. Add the garlic, pepper flakes, capers, and white wine, and cook for 1 minute, stirring.

Remove from the heat and add the chopped tomatoes, crabmeat, lemon juice, sea salt, pepper, and most of the parsley and basil, stirring.

Drain the pasta well and add to the crab mixture, along with an extra drizzle of olive oil. Toss well to coat.

Divide among four warm pasta plates, and scatter the remaining herbs and grated lemon zest over the top.

soba noodles with tobiko

I always keep dried soba (buckwheat) noodles in the pantry for this refreshing, light, chilled noodle salad. Tobiko (pronounced *tob-ee-ko*) is crunchy, tiny, flying fish roe, available from Japanese markets. You could also use salmon caviar.

SERVES 4

7 oz dried soba (Japanese buckwheat noodles)
sea salt
1 tbsp lemon juice
1 tsp sugar
3 tbsp Japanese soy sauce
3 tbsp mirin
2 oz tobiko or salmon caviar
1 tsp wasabi paste

Add the noodles to a large pan of boiling, salted water and cook until *al dente*—tender but still firm to the bite, 6 to 8 minutes. Drain well, rinse under cold running water, and chill for an hour or so.

Combine the lemon juice and sugar, stirring until the sugar has dissolved. Add the soy and mirin, stir, and chill for an hour or so.

When you are ready to serve, toss the noodles in the chilled sauce. Drain and toss with the tobiko, then divide among four chilled platters. Serve with wasabi paste, for those who like it hot.

tagliatelle with pumpkin & sage

This is a new look at Italy's lovely *tortelli di zucca*, which marries the natural sweetness of pumpkin with buttery, rich Parmesan in an almost medieval manner. Instead of pumpkin, you can use onion squash, butternut squash, or even sweet potato.

SERVES 4

1$^1/_4$ lb pumpkin

1 onion, peeled

3 tbsp butter

1$^1/_4$ cups vegetable or chicken stock

1 tsp sugar

pinch of grated nutmeg

sea salt and pepper

10 oz fine tagliatelle or fettuccine

1 tbsp olive oil

12 whole sage leaves, plus 6 roughly chopped leaves

$^1/_4$ cup freshly grated Parmesan, plus extra for serving

Roughly chop the pumpkin, cut off the peel and seeds, and cut into $^1/_2$-inch cubes. Halve and finely slice the onion.

Melt 2 tbsp butter in a frying pan, add the onion, and cook gently for 5 minutes. Add the pumpkin and toss well, then add the stock, sugar, nutmeg, and sea salt, and cook gently until tender, about 20 minutes. It should still be slightly soupy.

Add the pasta to a large pan of boiling, salted water and cook until *al dente*—tender but firm to the bite. Meanwhile, heat the olive oil in a small pan and gently fry the whole sage leaves until crisp.

Drain the pasta, then toss lightly with the pumpkin, adding the remaining 1 tbsp butter, chopped sage, Parmesan, and lots of pepper.

Divide among warm pasta bowls and scatter the crisp sage leaves on top. Serve with extra Parmesan at the table.

chicken & cilantro salad

This is a favorite salad of mine whenever I come home with some cooked chicken or duck from Chinatown, or have some leftover chicken from a roast.

SERVES 4

1 carrot, peeled

1/2 English cucumber, peeled

2 green onions, trimmed

3 tbsp lime juice

1 tsp sugar

sea salt and pepper

1 shallot, peeled and finely sliced

8 oz rice vermicelli noodles

2 cooked chicken breast halves

1 tbsp toasted sesame oil

1 tbsp fish sauce

3 tbsp cilantro leaves

1/2 mild red chili pepper, finely sliced

2 tbsp chopped roasted peanuts

Cut the carrot and cucumber into 4-inch sections. Finely slice lengthwise, then cut into fine matchsticks. Finely shred the green onions lengthwise.

Mix the lime juice with the sugar, sea salt, and pepper. Toss the carrot, cucumber, green onions, and shallot in the mixture and set aside.

Pour boiling water over the noodles and let soak for 6 to 7 minutes. Roughly shred the cooked chicken.

Drain the noodles, rinse in cold water, and drain again. Snip 2 or 3 times with scissors, then toss with the chicken, sesame oil, fish sauce, and cilantro leaves. Add the chili, shallot, green onions, cucumber, carrot, and lime dressing, and toss lightly.

Divide the salad among four serving bowls. Scatter the chopped peanuts over the top and serve.

spaghetti al bianco

When Italians feel the need to look after themselves, they cook "*al bianco*," or "white" food without the acidity of tomatoes. This lemon-scented "white" meat ragu has the power to make us all feel better.

SERVES 4

$^1/_3$ oz dried wild mushrooms
1 leek, trimmed
2 celery stalks
2 carrots, peeled
1 tbsp olive oil
1 tbsp butter
4 thyme sprigs
1 tbsp chopped parsley
$1^1/_2$ lb lean ground beef
1 tbsp all-purpose flour
sea salt and pepper
2 cups hot stock or water
14 oz spaghetti
1 tbsp grated lemon zest
freshly grated Parmesan for
  serving

Soak the dried mushrooms in 1 cup boiling water for 30 minutes. Finely slice the leek and celery, and finely dice the carrots.

Heat the olive oil and butter in a pan and cook the leek for 5 minutes. Add the carrots, celery, thyme, and parsley, and cook for 5 minutes. Add the beef and cook, stirring, until nicely browned. Sprinkle with the flour, sea salt, and pepper, and stir for a minute or two to cook the flour.

Add the mushrooms with their soaking water, discarding any sediment. Gradually stir in the hot stock or water, then simmer, partly covered, for 45 minutes or longer.

Cook the spaghetti in plenty of boiling, salted water until *al dente*— tender but firm to the bite. Drain well, then toss with the meat sauce and add the grated lemon zest. Serve with freshly grated Parmesan.

seafood

fish

seafood

fish

hangtown fry

This amazing omelet folded around breaded, fried oysters was supposedly created during the California Gold Rush of 1849, for a miner who had struck it rich. I've freshened it up for a fun, quick supper. Serve with hot sauce.

SERVES 2

4 bacon slices
6–8 large oysters, freshly
  shucked
1 tbsp all-purpose flour
sea salt and pepper
1 beaten egg for coating
2 tbsp fine dry bread crumbs
2 tbsp butter
6 eggs, beaten
1 tbsp minced parsley

Fry the bacon in a nonstick frying pan until crisp. Remove and set aside.

Reserve the oyster juices. Coat each oyster in flour, sea salt, and pepper, then in the beaten egg, then in the bread crumbs. Melt 1 tbsp butter in the pan and fry the oysters lightly until golden, turning once. Drain on paper towels. Wipe the pan clean.

Beat the 6 eggs with the oyster juices, sea salt, and pepper. Add the remaining 1 tbsp butter to the pan, then pour in the eggs and stir briskly for 30 seconds.

Stop stirring and let cook over medium heat, pulling back the edges as they set and tilting the pan to force the runny bits to the edges. When the omelet is almost set, add the oysters and parsley, and cook for 30 seconds longer.

Slide the omelet onto a warm plate, jerking the pan to help it fold in half. Serve half the omelet each, topped with the crisp bacon.

calamari with "taramasalata"

A heavenly combination of paprika-dusted calamari rings with a light, fluffy purée of smoked salmon that tastes even better than traditional Greek taramasalata made with smoked cod roe.

SERVES 4

1 lb fresh squid (calamari),
   cleaned
^{2}/$_3$ cup all-purpose flour
^{1}/$_2$ tsp paprika
sea salt and pepper
3 tbsp olive oil
2 tbsp salmon roe

"TARAMASALATA"

4 oz smoked salmon,
   chopped
1 cup cream cheese
^{1}/$_2$ cup thick plain yogurt
2 tsp drained white horseradish
1 tbsp lemon juice

To make the "taramasalata," combine the smoked salmon, cream cheese, yogurt, horseradish, lemon juice, and freshly ground pepper in a food processor. Process to combine, then refrigerate until required.

Cut the squid tubes into ^{1}/$_2$-inch rings, and the tentacles into smaller sections. Mix the flour with the paprika, 1 tsp salt, and ^{1}/$_2$ tsp pepper. Toss the squid pieces in the flour, then shake off the excess.

Heat half the olive oil in a frying pan until hot. Quickly fry the squid in batches, turning once, for about 30 seconds. Remove and drain on paper towels, adding a little extra oil to the pan for each batch.

Spoon the "taramasalata" into four small pots and top with salmon roe. Serve with the fried calamari.

garlic-sizzled shrimp

There is normal food, and then there is vacation food. Vacation food in Spain means sitting in the sun drinking chilled white wine, nibbling on olives and bread, while you wait for the much-loved tapas dish of *gambas* (big shrimp) sizzled with the right amount of *ajillo* (garlic) and served in the still-sizzling pan.

SERVES 4

1 lb raw jumbo shrimp
sea salt and pepper
3 garlic cloves, crushed
1 small, hot red chili pepper, chopped, or pinch of dried red pepper flakes
1/2 tsp Spanish paprika
2 tbsp Spanish sherry
3 tbsp olive oil
1 tbsp torn parsley leaves

Peel the shrimp, leaving the tails, and pat dry. Devein each shrimp by threading a thin bamboo skewer through the back of the "neck" and hooking out any black thread. Season with sea salt, and place the shrimp in a small frying pan that you can take to the table.

Combine the crushed garlic, chili, paprika, sherry, and olive oil, and spoon over the shrimp. Let marinate for 10 minutes or longer.

Place the frying pan over high heat and cook, shaking the pan to turn the shrimp, until they change color and the garlic is lightly golden, about 3 minutes. The sherry will probably catch and flame, so be careful.

Sprinkle with the parsley, sea salt, and pepper, and serve while still sizzling, with plenty of bread to mop up the garlicky juices.

extra

garlicky, golden aïoli
A thick, lush, creamy mayonnaise that adds a silky richness to anything it touches.

to make it work 2 egg yolks, 1 crushed garlic clove, 1/2 tsp salt, 1 tsp Dijon mustard, and 2 tbsp lemon juice in a blender or food processor. Very slowly, at a bare trickle, add 7 tbsp sunflower or vegetable oil, then 7 tbsp olive oil, blending until thick, smooth, and silky. Blend in 1 tbsp boiling water, then refrigerate.

serve aïoli with garlicky shrimp, seafood soups, grilled fish, asparagus, hard-boiled eggs, roast pork, tomato salads, and vegetable stews.

salmon in light, fragrant broth

You can ruin the richness of salmon by teaming it with rich sauces, cream, or mayonnaise. It doesn't need them. Instead, bathe it in a gentle, fragrant broth of Thai aromatics with a little kick of lime juice, and serve with steamed rice.

SERVES 4

4 salmon fillets, about
    5 oz each
3 tbsp fish sauce
2 lemon grass stalks, trimmed
2 shallots, peeled
1 small, hot red chili pepper
5 oz mushrooms (oyster,
    shiitake, or button)
4 oz baby spinach leaves
2 cups chicken or vegetable
    stock
1 tsp sugar
1 tbsp vegetable oil
sea salt and pepper
1 tbsp lime juice

Toss the salmon in 1 tbsp fish sauce and set aside. Peel the lemon grass stalks and finely slice the white part. Finely slice the shallots, chili, and mushrooms. Wash the spinach and drain.

Heat the stock in a saucepan with the lemon grass, shallots, chili, mushrooms, and sugar, and simmer for 10 minutes.

Heat the oil in a nonstick frying pan and sear the salmon, skin-side down, until the skin is crisp, about 3 minutes. Turn and lightly sear the other side for 1 minute, leaving the inside pink. Season with salt and pepper.

Add the spinach to the hot broth for 10 seconds until barely wilted, then remove with tongs. Divide the spinach among four warm, shallow bowls and place the salmon on top.

Add the remaining 2 tbsp fish sauce and the lime juice to the broth, and spoon it around the salmon. Serve with a bowl of rice alongside.

portuguese fish stew

This wet, soupy rice overflowing with fish, shrimp, and chorizo sausage is my favorite Portuguese vacation food. If you make it ahead, the rice will absorb the stock, so keep some extra stock handy and add it before serving.

SERVES 4

1$^1/_4$ lb thick, firm, white fish
    fillets, skinned
4 tbsp olive oil
8 raw jumbo shrimp in shells
sea salt and pepper
2 smoked chorizo sausages
1 red bell pepper
1 onion, peeled
3 garlic cloves, minced
2 large tomatoes, chopped
5 cups hot fish stock
1$^3/_4$ cups risotto rice
1 tsp Spanish paprika
2 bay leaves
2 tbsp torn flat-leaf parsley
1 lemon, quartered

Cut the fish into generous bite-sized pieces. Heat half the olive oil in a frying pan and cook the fish and shrimp on all sides until they just change color. Remove to a plate and season well.

Slice the chorizo sausages. Finely chop the red pepper, discarding the core and seeds. Halve and slice the onion. Heat the remaining olive oil in the pan and fry the onion, garlic, red pepper, and chorizo slices for 10 minutes, stirring well.

Add the tomatoes and stock, and bring to a boil. Add the rice, paprika, bay leaves, sea salt, and pepper, stirring well. Reduce the heat to very low, cover, and simmer until the rice is almost cooked but still wet and soupy, about 20 minutes (add more stock if not soupy).

Add the fish and shrimp, and simmer gently for 10 minutes. Scatter the torn parsley over and serve in warm pasta bowls, with lemon wedges for squeezing.

a bag of shellfish

This is a great way of cooking up a mess of shellfish, the foil bag keeping all the flavor—and the nutrients—trapped inside. Make sure you have plenty of kitchen foil before you start, or you will be caught short.

SERVES 4

14 oz small hardshell clams in shell
14 oz mussels in shell
12 raw large shrimp in shell, deveined
12 cherry tomatoes, halved
12 small black olives
1 hot red chili pepper, finely sliced
4 garlic cloves, flattened
1/4 cup extra virgin olive oil
1 tbsp chopped parsley
sea salt and pepper
1 lemon, quartered

Heat the oven to 450°F. To make the oven bags, cut four 18-inch-long sheets of wide kitchen foil. Fold in half end to end, then crimp the sides together, leaving the top open.

Scrub the clams and mussels, and pull out the beards from mussels. (Discard any clams and mussels that are not closed or that have cracked shells.) Toss the shrimp, clams, and mussels in a big bowl with the tomatoes, olives, chili, garlic, olive oil, parsley, sea salt, and pepper.

Divide the shellfish mixture among the four parcels. Seal the tops by crimping tightly, so that no air can escape. Place in a roasting pan and bake for 15 minutes or until the bags puff up like balloons.

Carefully open and slide the contents and their juices onto warm serving plates. Serve with lemon wedges, crusty bread, and fingerbowls.

mexican baked fish

If you like pickled jalapeño peppers—and you're mad if you don't—then you'll love this fish, baked Veracruz-style, under a rich sauce of onion, garlic, tomato, capers, olives, and fiery jalapeños.

SERVES 4

4 thick, firm, white fish fillets,
   6 oz each, skinned
1 tbsp lime juice
$^1/_2$ tsp sea salt
1 onion, peeled
1 red bell pepper
3 tbsp olive oil, plus extra
   for pan
1 garlic clove, finely sliced
14-oz can tomatoes, chopped
10 green olives, pitted
1 tbsp salted capers, rinsed
1 tbsp pickled jalapeños
pinch of cayenne pepper
1 bay leaf
cilantro leaves for garnish

Heat the oven to 400°F. Rub the fish with the lime juice and sea salt, and set aside.

Finely slice the onion into rings. Cut the red pepper into strips, discarding the core and seeds. Heat 2 tbsp olive oil in a frying pan, and cook the onion until soft and pale, about 10 minutes. Add the garlic and cook for 1 minute longer.

Add the tomatoes, red pepper, and $^2/_3$ cup water, stirring. Add the green olives, capers, jalapeños, cayenne, and bay leaf. Cook gently until the red pepper is tender, 10 to 15 minutes.

Heat 1 tbsp olive oil in a frying pan and sear the fish fillets for 1 minute on each side, then transfer to an oiled baking pan. Spoon the sauce on top and bake until the fish is cooked through, 15 to 20 minutes, depending on thickness. Scatter the cilantro over and serve with rice.

tamarind fish curry

What makes this simple fish curry special is the citrus tang of tamarind, extracted from the pulp of the tamarind pod. Find tamarind concentrate or purée in good supermarkets and Asian markets.

SERVES 4

1$^1/_2$ lb salmon fillets, skinned
1 tsp sea salt
1 onion, peeled
2 tbsp vegetable oil
$^3/_4$-inch piece of ginger
1 garlic clove, crushed
1 tsp ground coriander
1 tsp ground cumin
$^1/_2$ tsp ground turmeric
2 small, hot red chili peppers, sliced
1 tbsp tamarind concentrate
1 tbsp tomato paste
1$^3/_4$ cups coconut milk
1 tsp sugar
torn cilantro leaves for garnish

Cut the salmon into bite-sized chunks. Rub with $^1/_2$ tsp salt and set aside.

Halve and finely slice the onion. Heat the oil in a heavy-based pan and fry the onion until soft but not colored. Peel and grate the ginger. Add to the pan along with the garlic and fry for 1 minute longer, stirring.

Add the ground coriander, cumin, turmeric, and chilies, stirring well until fragrant. Add the tamarind, tomato paste, coconut milk, 1 cup water, $^1/_2$ tsp salt, and the sugar, and heat gently, stirring. Simmer, uncovered, for about 10 minutes. Taste and adjust for tamarind and chili.

Add the fish and simmer until cooked, about 5 minutes. Scatter some cilantro over and serve with steamed rice.

lime

The lime is the exotic, tropical cousin of the everyday lemon: stronger, sweeter, and more fashionable. For an instant lime sauce, add lime wedges to the roasting pan with chicken or lamb, or cook sliced limes alongside grilled or pan-fried fish—the limes soften and spill out warm tangy juices to make an instant sauce.

lime butter Blend 2 tbsp grated lime zest and $1/2$ tsp sea salt into 7 tbsp soft butter. Wrap in a bonbon of foil, twisting the ends tightly, and freeze for 1 hour. Unwrap, slice, and serve on grilled or pan-fried fish.

avocado & lime whip Halve, pit, and peel an avocado, then blend in a food processor with 2 tbsp lime juice, a dash of hot sauce, and sea salt until smooth. Spoon onto rice crackers and top with lime zest.

pork with lime & mint In a wok, combine 10 oz ground pork, 2 tbsp fish sauce, 1 finely sliced hot red chili pepper, and 7 tbsp water. Cook, stirring, until the water is absorbed, about 10 minutes. Add a squeeze of lime juice and a handful of mint leaves. Serve in lettuce leaves.

cucumber & lime smash Cut 2 limes into quarters and pound to a pulp with 2 tbsp sugar. Divide between 2 tall glasses. Add 2 fl oz vodka to each with finely sliced cucumber, mint leaves, and crushed ice, then fill with tonic water.

lime & coconut macaroons Use your hands to mix $1/2$ cup sugar, 2 cups unsweetened dried coconut, 2 egg whites, 1 tbsp grated lime zest, and 1 tbsp lime juice to a thick paste. Press into a flat square $1/2$ inch high. Cut out small rounds and bake on a cookie sheet at 325°F until lightly golden, 12 to 15 minutes.

salt-baked fish

Sea bass is the classic choice, but this method is also brilliant with snapper, salmon, gurnard, or any large, round-bodied fish. If your fish is larger than this, bake for 10 minutes per pound, plus an extra 10 minutes. And don't forget to show off the fish at the table before you crack open the salt crust.

SERVES 4

1 sea bass, about 2³/₄ lb,
  scaled and cleaned
3 rosemary sprigs
10 thyme sprigs
2 bay leaves
2 garlic cloves, smashed flat
4 egg whites
4¹/₂ lb coarse sea or kosher salt
extra virgin olive oil for serving
1 lemon, quartered

Heat the oven to 350°F. Rinse the fish and pat dry. Stuff the rosemary, thyme, bay leaves, and garlic into the cavity. Beat the egg whites until they form soft peaks, fold in the salt, and mix well.

Lightly oil a nonstick baking sheet. Arrange half the salt mixture in a ¹/₂-inch layer across the middle, roughly to the same shape as the fish but a little wider. Place the fish on top. Pack the remaining salt mixture over the fish to cover it completely. Bake until the crust has turned golden, about 30 minutes, then let rest for 10 minutes.

Crack open the crust and gently transfer the fish to a warmed, large serving platter, brushing off any excess salt. Peel off any skin (sometimes it lifts off with the crust), then serve the fish with a drizzle of extra virgin olive oil and lemon wedges.

chicken

pork

chicken

pork

turkey with chorizo & lemon

The ultimate celebration package for everything from a birthday buffet dinner to Christmas Day: a golden, roasted breast of turkey rolled around a stuffing of spicy chorizo sausage, lemon, and herbs.

SERVES 6

10 oz fresh chorizo sausage
1 boneless turkey breast,
   about 2³/₄ lb
sea salt and pepper
1 tbsp finely grated lemon zest
¹/₂ cup freshly grated
   Parmesan
¹/₂ tsp freshly grated nutmeg
1 tbsp minced parsley
1 tbsp minced thyme
1 egg, beaten
2 cups fresh white bread crumbs
1 lemon, sliced
1³/₄ cups dry white wine,
   stock, or water

To make the stuffing, skin the chorizo sausages. Pinch the meat into a frying pan and cook for 5 minutes, then cool. Heat the oven to 400°F.

To butterfly the turkey breast, lay skin-side down on a board and make a shallow cut down the center of the meat, then cut horizontally through the thick meat on either side and open it up like a book. Cover with plastic wrap and bash it flat with a rolling pin, then rub with sea salt and pepper.

Lightly mix the cooled chorizo with the lemon zest, Parmesan, nutmeg, parsley, thyme, egg, and bread crumbs.

Form the stuffing into a sausage on top of the turkey. Roll tightly, tuck in the ends, and tie securely with string. Season well.

Place the turkey roll, skin-side up, in a roasting pan and arrange the lemon slices on top. Add the wine to the pan, and roast for 1 hour and 10 minutes. Let rest for 10 minutes, then remove the string and carve thickly. Serve with the cooking juices.

bang bang chicken

Why bang bang? Apparently, Sichuan street vendors sold this as a snack, first hammering the chicken with a "bang," or wooden cudgel, to loosen the fibers.

SERVES 4

2 chicken breast halves
2 slices peeled fresh ginger
4 green onions, trimmed
$^{1}/_{2}$ English cucumber, peeled
1 carrot, peeled
2 celery stalks
1 tsp toasted sesame oil
1 tsp rice wine vinegar
1 tsp sesame seeds, toasted

SAUCE

1 tbsp toasted sesame oil
2 tbsp peanut butter
1 tbsp sweet chili sauce
2 tbsp soy sauce
2 tsp sugar
1 tbsp rice wine vinegar
1 small, hot red chili pepper

Put the chicken into a pan with 1 tsp salt, the ginger, and enough cold water to cover. Finely shred the green onions and add half to the pan. Bring to a simmer and poach gently for 15 minutes. Remove from the heat and leave for 30 minutes, then drain.

Cut the cucumber, carrot, and celery into matchsticks. Finely shred the chicken and combine with the cucumber, carrot, celery, and remaining green onions. Add the sesame oil, vinegar, sea salt, and pepper, and toss to mix. Arrange in four bowls or platters.

To make the sauce, mix the sesame oil, peanut butter, chili sauce, soy, sugar, and vinegar to a paste. Gradually whisk in up to $^{1}/_{2}$ cup water until runny but still quite thick. Finely slice the chili pepper and stir in.

Spoon the sauce over the chicken and vegetables, sprinkle with toasted sesame seeds, and serve, with chopsticks.

honey

Golden, luscious honey makes everyone's life that little bit sweeter. Like wines, there are honey varietals, made from single flowers as opposed to blends, so find the ones you like and use different honeys for different reasons. To measure honey, use a honey twirler, or dip your spoon in hot water first, and the honey will slip and slide off the spoon easily.

honey figs Halve 4 figs, lay on foil, and drizzle with 1 tbsp honey. Broil for 5 minutes and serve with a creamy blue cheese and oat crackers.

honey-roast pork Cut 1 lb pork tenderloin into 6-inch lengths. Marinate in 2 tbsp honey, 2 tbsp hoisin sauce, 2 tbsp soy sauce, and $1/2$ tsp five-spice powder for 1 hour. Roast on a rack set over a pan of water at 425°F for 30 minutes, basting occasionally. Slice and serve with rice or noodles, or toss in a stir-fry.

honey sausages Roast your favorite pork sausages until crisp-skinned. Drizzle with 2 tbsp honey and a squeeze of lemon juice. Amazing.

honey, ginger & lemon tea To ease a sore throat, put a slice of fresh ginger, a slice of lemon, and 1 tbsp honey in a heatproof glass and pour boiling water over. Stir and sip.

honey lassi Blend 1 cup mixed berries and 1 tbsp honey in a blender until smooth, then spoon into chilled glasses. Blend 1 cup plain yogurt with 2 tbsp honey and 6 ice cubes, pour on top, and gently stir.

honey-roast pears Heat 2 tbsp butter with 2 tbsp honey in a frying pan, stirring. Peel and halve 2 pears, add to the pan, and cook, spooning the sauce over the pears, until caramelized. Serve with a glass of sweet wine.

maple-roast pork

This is a typically gutsy, clever "gastropub" dish, adapted from a recipe by chef Steve Harris of The Sportsman pub near Whitstable on the English coast.

SERVES 4

1 tbsp smoked paprika
$1/4$ cup maple syrup
3 tbsp vegetable oil
4 large pork loin chops,
   about 8 oz each
2 tbsp mayonnaise
1 tbsp grainy mustard
8 oz greens or spinach
sea salt and pepper
1 tbsp butter
squeeze of lemon juice

Mix the paprika, maple syrup, and 2 tbsp of the oil together in a bowl, then rub into the pork chops. Cover and refrigerate for as long as you have, be it an hour or overnight.

Heat the oven to 325°F. Heat the remaining oil in a frying pan, and gently fry the chops on both sides until they start to blacken (be careful, as the rendered fat might spit). Using tongs, hold each chop at right angles in the pan to color the edge as well, then transfer to a baking dish. Cook in the oven until tender, about 25 minutes.

Mix the mayonnaise and mustard together and set aside.

Wash and dry the greens and shred finely. Cook in a little boiling, salted water until tender, then drain thoroughly. Dress with the butter, lemon juice, and sea salt and pepper to taste.

Spoon the cooking juices over the chops and season well. Serve with the greens and mustard mayonnaise.

claypot chicken

This uses my magic marinade—magic, because whatever meat is left in it becomes magically tender. Traditionally this would have been cooked in a claypot, but you can use any sort of pot or pan.

SERVES 4

10 dried black mushrooms (shiitake)

1 lb boneless chicken thighs

$^2/_3$ cup canned bamboo shoots

4 green onions, trimmed

10 oz firm tofu, drained

2 thick slices of peeled ginger

2 tbsp vegetable oil

1 tbsp Chinese rice wine

2 tbsp soy sauce

1 tsp sugar

2 tsp cornstarch

MAGIC MARINADE:

2 tbsp soy sauce

1 tsp toasted sesame oil

1 tsp cornstarch

Soak the mushrooms in 1 cup boiling water for 30 minutes. Cut the chicken into generous bite-sized pieces. For the marinade, combine the soy, sesame oil, and cornstarch in a bowl. Add the chicken, turn to coat, and let marinate for 20 minutes.

Drain the mushrooms, reserving 7 fl oz water, and finely slice, discarding stems. Finely slice the bamboo shoots. Cut the green onions on the diagonal into 2-inch lengths. Cut the tofu into $^3/_4$-inch cubes. Cut the ginger into matchsticks.

Heat the oil in a wok or wide cooking pot, and stir-fry the ginger and chicken for 2 minutes. Add the mushrooms, bamboo shoots, and green onions, and stir-fry for 2 minutes. Add the mushroom water, rice wine, soy, and sugar, and bring to a boil. Add the tofu. Simmer for 15 minutes.

Mix the 2 tsp cornstarch with 1 tbsp cold water and add to the wok, stirring well until the sauce thickens. Serve with rice.

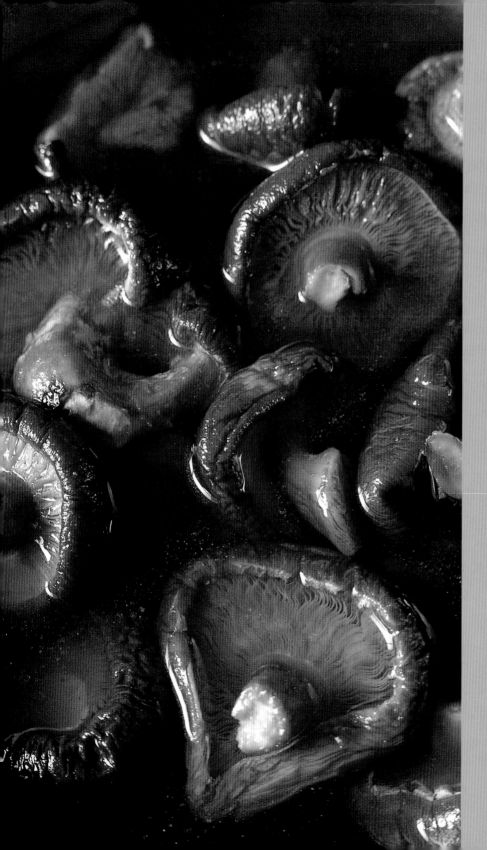

extra

dried mushrooms

With a pack of dried black (shiitake) mushrooms, you are just a soak away from great stocks and sauces.

mushroom stock
Soak 6 dried mushrooms in 1 cup boiling water for 30 minutes. Pick out the mushrooms and slice finely, discarding stems. Strain stock through a fine sieve. Use stock and mushrooms in soups, stir-fries, risotto, and sauces.

shiitake sauce
Heat the sliced mushrooms and their stock with 1 tbsp each soy, hoisin, and oyster sauces. Mix 2 tsp cornstarch and 1 tbsp Chinese rice wine to a smooth paste, and stir into the mushroom mixture. Simmer, stirring, until it thickens. Serve spooned over pan-fried pork, fish, or chicken.

broiled pork balls with mint

Vietnamese cooking is light, fresh, and healthy, and, as its defining characteristic, uses basket-loads of fresh herbs and salad greens. These meatballs (*nem nuong*) are typically light and lovely.

SERVES 4

1 tbsp Thai fragrant or jasmine rice (raw, not washed)
14 oz ground pork
2 garlic cloves, crushed
sea salt and pepper
1 tbsp fish sauce
1 tbsp sugar
8 oz dried rice vermicelli
2 tbsp mint leaves
1 head iceberg lettuce, chilled

DRESSING

1 tsp sugar
2 tbsp lime juice
3 tbsp fish sauce
2 tbsp chopped mint
1 hot red or green chili pepper

Soak 8 bamboo skewers in water. Dry-fry the rice in a small frying pan until lightly golden, then grind to a powder.

Combine the pork, ground rice, garlic, $1/2$ tsp sea salt, $1/4$ tsp pepper, the fish sauce, and sugar, and knead until well mixed. With wet hands, shape the mixture into around 24 small balls, each the size of a walnut.

Cook the noodles in boiling water for 2 to 3 minutes, drain, and rinse in cold water.

To make the dressing, mix the sugar with the lime juice, then add the fish sauce and mint. Slice the chili. Toss the noodles and chili in the dressing.

Heat the broiler. Drain the skewers and thread the pork balls onto them, three to a skewer. Broil, turning occasionally, until golden brown all over, about 5 minutes. Serve with the noodle salad, extra mint leaves, and lettuce leaves for wrapping.

provençal garlic chicken

This is the ultimate garlic dish, based on the classic pot-roasted chicken with forty cloves of garlic. Serve with a green salad of small leaves and herbs, with a tablespoonful of the cooking juices whisked into the vinaigrette.

SERVES 4

1 organic chicken, around 3 lb
sea salt and pepper
2 bay leaves
few thyme sprigs
$1/4$ cup olive oil, plus extra for casserole
40 plump whole garlic cloves, unpeeled
8 or 12 small new potatoes, unpeeled
5 tbsp dry white wine

Heat the oven to 350°F. Rub the chicken with a little salt, pop the bay leaves and 2 thyme sprigs inside, and truss with string.

Place in a lightly oiled, large, lidded casserole and add the garlic cloves, potatoes, and white wine. Drizzle the olive oil over the chicken, scatter a few thyme sprigs on top, and season well with sea salt and pepper.

Lay a sheet of foil across the casserole, clamp the lid on tightly, and pot-roast for $1^{1}/_4$ hours. Remove the lid and increase the heat to 425°F. Roast until the skin is golden and the chicken is cooked through, 10 to 15 minutes longer.

Gently transfer the chicken to a serving platter, remove the string, and carve. Pile the garlic cloves on top of the chicken and serve with the potatoes and cooking juices. Squish the garlic and eat the sweet, nutty purée with the chicken.

mustard chicken wings

Mustard, honey, and lemon juice combine to give chicken wings a golden suntan and a real flavor kick. Serve as an easy, no-fuss lunch or supper, or cool and pack for a picnic.

SERVES 4

8 chicken wings
1 tbsp honey
2 tbsp Dijon mustard
2 tsp lemon juice
sea salt and pepper
2 bunches watercress
1 orange
4 crisp baby radishes
1 tsp olive oil
1 tbsp balsamic vinegar

Trim the chicken wings and pat dry. Mix the honey, mustard, lemon juice, sea salt, and pepper in a bowl, and toss the wings well until coated. Let marinate for 30 minutes.

Heat the oven to 400°F. Place the chicken wings on a rack set above a foil-lined pan (to prevent the drips from burning) and bake until sticky and golden, about 30 minutes.

Meanwhile, trim the watercress, wash, and spin dry. Peel the orange thickly, removing the white pith, and cut into sections. Finely slice the radishes. Toss the watercress, orange, and radishes in the olive oil and balsamic vinegar.

Serve the hot chicken wings with the orange and watercress salad.

chinese spare ribs

If it's summer, you can toss these on the grill. If it isn't, then cook them in the oven, and they will still end up gloriously caramelized and sticky. To turn them into a meal, serve with rice and Chinese greens.

SERVES 4

2 $1/4$ lb long pork spare ribs

MARINADE

2 tsp Chinese five-spice powder

$2/3$ cup hoisin sauce

2 tbsp ketchup

3 tbsp Chinese rice wine or dry sherry

$1/2$ tsp sea salt

1 tbsp freshly grated ginger

DIPPING SAUCE

2 tbsp hoisin sauce

1 tbsp sweet chili sauce

1 tbsp soy sauce

For the marinade, combine the five-spice powder, hoisin, ketchup, rice wine, salt, and ginger in a bowl and mix thoroughly. Cut the pork into individual ribs, add to the marinade, and turn to coat thoroughly. Let marinate for 2 hours or overnight, tossing occasionally.

Heat the oven to 450°F. Place the ribs on a rack set over a baking pan containing 1 cup water. Bake for 20 minutes, then turn the ribs over, lower the oven setting to 400°F, and cook for 15 to 20 minutes longer. Keep an eye on the ribs—you want them scorched and sizzling, but not burnt to a frazzle.

For the dipping sauce, combine the hoisin, sweet chili, and soy sauces. Remove the spare ribs from the oven and serve with the dipping sauce.

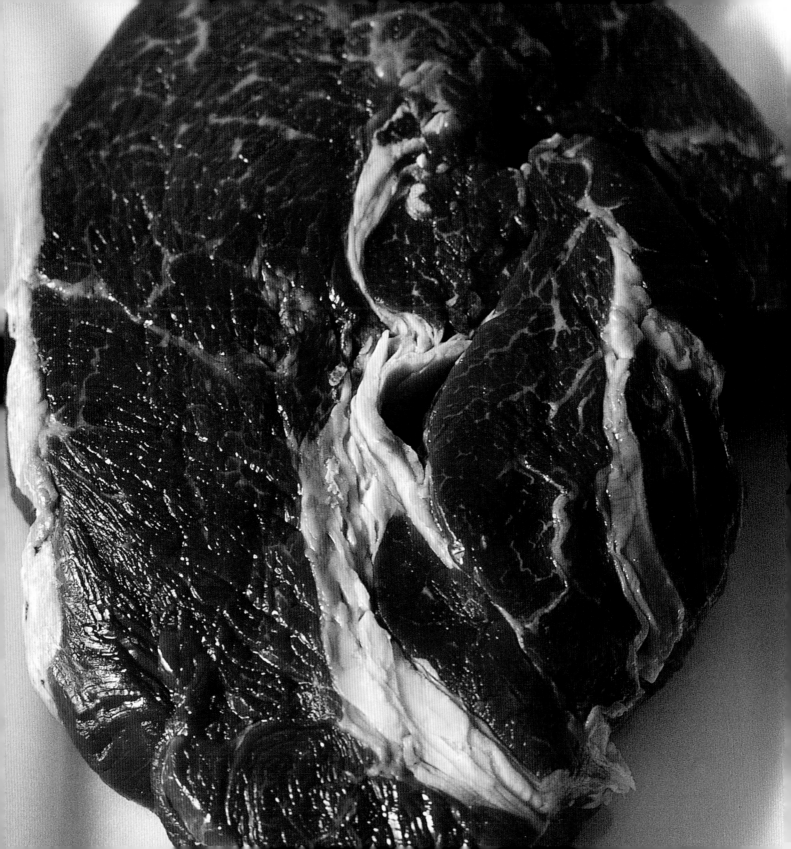

beef

lamb

lamb

beef

beef & beer stew

This wonderfully rich stew is based on the famous Flemish carbonnade, of beef braised in beer with plenty of onions. The secret is to brown your meat really well to begin with.

SERVES 4 TO 6

2 1/4 lb boneless beef, such as shoulder or chuck
2 tbsp all-purpose flour
sea salt and pepper
1 1/4 lb small white onions
2 tbsp olive oil
2 tbsp butter
1 tbsp tomato paste
2 bay leaves
1 tbsp Dijon mustard
1 tbsp brown sugar
1 3/4 cups lager
1 1/4 cups boiling stock or water
2 tbsp torn flat-leaf parsley

Heat the oven to 300°F. Cut the beef into large cubes, and coat lightly in the flour, sea salt, and pepper. Peel the onions, keeping the root, then cut through the root into thick wedges.

Heat half the oil and butter in a large stovetop-to-oven casserole. Brown the meat in batches, on all sides, removing to a plate when browned.

Add the remaining oil and butter to the casserole and cook the onions until soft, about 10 minutes. Add the tomato paste, bay leaves, mustard, sugar, salt, and pepper, stirring. Gradually add the lager, stirring constantly, followed by the boiling stock or water.

Return the beef to the casserole and bring to a simmer. Cover and cook in the oven (or gently on the stovetop, if preferred), stirring occasionally, for 2 1/2 to 3 hours. Sprinkle with the parsley and serve with mashed potato and something green.

lamb sirloin & green onion mash

This is a brilliant mini-roast. Ask your butcher to bone four large lamb sirloin chops, cut from the upper leg. The meat has a wonderful flavor.

SERVES 4

4–6 anchovy fillets
4 thick, boneless lamb sirloin
(upper leg) chops, about
7 oz each
sea salt and pepper
a little olive oil
8 oz cherry tomatoes
GREEN ONION MASH
1$^{1}/_{4}$ lb potatoes, peeled
1 tbsp butter
6 green onions, minced
$^{1}/_{4}$ cup milk
freshly grated nutmeg

Heat the oven to 425°F. Arrange the anchovy fillets on the "inside" of each boned chop, season well, roll up, and tie into shape with string. Brush with olive oil and sear in a hot pan until well browned all over.

Toss the cherry tomatoes in olive oil, place in a roasting pan, and roast for 10 minutes. Add the lamb mini-roasts to the pan. Roast for 15 minutes for medium rare, removing the tomatoes when soft and squishy.

Meanwhile, cut the potatoes into chunks and cook in boiling, salted water until tender, about 20 minutes.

Let the lamb rest for 10 minutes under a loose sheet of foil. Drain the potatoes, add the butter, and mash. Beat in the green onions, milk, and grated nutmeg, plus sea salt and pepper to taste.

Remove the string and thickly slice the lamb. Serve with the green onion mash and roasted tomatoes, and drizzled with the roasting juices.

fast greek lamb with feta

Marinate your lamb in garlic, oregano, lemon juice, and olive oil, then quickly sear until hot and scorchy. Wrap it in warm pita bread with yogurt and feta, and serve with lemon wedges and a cold beer.

SERVES 4

1¹/₂ lb boneless lamb loin or
  leg steaks
1 tsp dried oregano
1 tbsp thyme leaves
4 pita breads
4 tbsp thick plain yogurt
4 oz feta cheese, crumbled
1 lemon, quartered
MARINADE
2 garlic cloves, crushed
2 tbsp olive oil
¹/₂ tsp dried oregano
1 tbsp lemon juice
sea salt and pepper

Slice the lamb finely but roughly, at different angles (basically, hack it to bits). For the marinade, combine the garlic, olive oil, oregano, lemon juice, sea salt, and pepper in a bowl. Add the lamb, turn to coat, and let marinate until ready to cook.

Heat a nonstick frying pan and sear the lamb over a high heat, tossing it in the pan until crisped on the edges, but still a little pink inside. Add the oregano and thyme, and toss well.

Heat the pita bread in a warm oven or dry frying pan for 3 minutes. Place a pita on each plate. Add a spoonful of yogurt, pile the lamb on top, and scatter the feta over. Serve with lemon quarters for squeezing.

roast peppered beef

The dinner party classic returns, this time with a peppery crust and a light red wine and horseradish sauce. Beautiful beef like this is worth the expense—and worth cracking open a great bottle of red.

SERVES 6 TO 8

1 beef tenderloin roast,
   about 4 lb
1 tbsp all-purpose flour
2 tbsp Dijon mustard
sea salt
1 tbsp cracked black pepper
a little olive oil for the pan
$1/2$ cup red wine
$1/2$ cup chicken stock
1 tbsp drained white
   horseradish
1 tbsp cold butter, diced
2 bunches of watercress,
   washed

Heat the oven to 450°F. Tuck in the tail end of the beef and tie with string to keep an even shape. Mix the flour, mustard, and $1/2$ tsp sea salt together to a paste, and spread over the beef with your hands. Scatter on the cracked pepper.

Place the tenderloin in an oiled roasting pan and roast for 15 minutes, then reduce the heat to 400°F. For rare to medium rare meat, roast for about 25 minutes longer. Transfer the beef to a warm plate, cover loosely with foil, and let rest for 15 minutes while you make the sauce.

Put the roasting pan over a medium heat. Add the wine and bring to a boil, scraping up any beefy juices. Add the stock and bring to a boil. Strain into a small pan and add any juices from the resting beef. Whisk in the horseradish, butter, and sea salt to taste, and keep warm.

Carve the beef thickly and arrange on six warm dinner plates with the watercress. Serve with the red wine and horseradish sauce.

extra

rare roast beef
Turn your leftover beef into world-class eating.

beef rolls with daikon
Top 10 slices of rare roast beef with grated daikon. Roll up, drizzle with toasted sesame oil, and sprinkle with Japanese togarashi pepper.

rare beef tonnata
Blend 4 oz good tuna with 3 anchovy fillets, 1 tbsp lemon juice, 1 tbsp rinsed salted capers, and 2/3 cup mayonnaise. Drizzle over thinly sliced roast beef.

thai beef salad
Mix together 2 tbsp lime juice, 2 tbsp Thai fish sauce, 1 tsp sugar, and 1 tsp toasted sesame oil. Toss with strips of rare roast beef and lots of basil, mint, and cilantro leaves.

steak tartare burgers

Take the ingredients of the traditional raw steak tartare, mix with your hands, form into burgers, and sear in a pan until crusty, and as rare as you dare.

SERVES 2

14 oz lean ground steak
1 egg yolk, beaten
3 anchovy fillets, chopped
1 shallot, peeled and minced
2 cornichons or cocktail
  gherkins, minced
2 tsp salted capers, rinsed
1 tsp Dijon mustard
dash of hot pepper sauce
1 tbsp chopped parsley
sea salt and pepper
1 tbsp olive oil
2 fresh English muffins
few arugula leaves for serving

In a bowl, combine the ground steak with the egg yolk, anchovy fillets, shallot, cornichons, capers, mustard, pepper sauce, parsley, sea salt, and pepper, mixing and mulching it well with your hands.

Shape the meat into two large, thick patties. Heat the olive oil in a heavy frying pan and sear the burgers on one side until dark and crusty, about 4 minutes. Turn the burgers over and cook the other side briefly, keeping them as rare as you like.

Heat the broiler. Split the muffins and toast lightly under the broiler. Place each burger on a muffin base, top with a few arugula leaves, and lean the muffin top against it. Serve with Dijon mustard or ketchup.

moorish lamb shanks

Long, slow cooking on the bone means meltingly tender meat in a rich, spicy, saffron-scented, Spanish-inspired stew.

SERVES 4

2 onions, peeled
4 carrots, peeled
2 celery stalks
4 lamb shanks, well trimmed
sea salt and pepper
all-purpose flour for dusting
2 tbsp olive oil
1 cup dry white wine
1 tsp Spanish smoked paprika
large pinch of ground saffron
2 tbsp tomato paste
14-oz can crushed tomatoes
1 red bell pepper
14-oz can chickpeas, drained
2 tsp torn flat-leaf parsley

Roughly chop the onions and carrots, and slice the celery. Dust the lamb shanks in flour seasoned with salt and pepper.

Heat the olive oil in a large frying pan or casserole. Add the lamb shanks and brown well on all sides, then remove to a plate.

Add the onions, carrots, and celery to the pan and cook, moving them around occasionally, until they start to soften, about 10 minutes. Add the wine and let it bubble and evaporate. Add the paprika, saffron, tomato paste, tomatoes, and 1 tsp salt, stirring well.

Return the lamb shanks to the pan, and add enough water to almost cover the bones. Cover and simmer gently for 1 hour.

Roughly chop the red pepper, discarding the core and seeds. Add to the pan along with the chickpeas and cook until the lamb shanks are tender and the whole thing is stewy rather than soupy, about 1 hour longer. Taste for salt and pepper, scatter the parsley leaves over, and serve.

new york meatloaf

How clever is this—a hand-formed meatloaf that comes with a built-in tomato sauce. Serve hot, or cool and serve in huge bread rolls for lunch.

SERVES 4

4 slices bread, crusts removed
$1/2$ cup milk
1 leek, trimmed
1 red bell pepper
1 lb ground beef
8 oz pork sausage meat
2 tbsp minced parsley
sea salt and pepper
$1/2$ tsp cayenne pepper
$1/4$ tsp grated nutmeg
2 tbsp ketchup
2 tsp Worcestershire sauce
  or Dijon mustard
1 egg, beaten
14-oz can crushed tomatoes
6 cherry tomatoes, halved
$1/2$ tsp dried oregano

Heat the oven to 400°F. Soak the bread in the milk for a minute or two, then lightly squeeze dry. Mince the leek. Mince the red pepper, discarding the core and seeds.

Combine the bread, beef, sausage meat, leek, red pepper, parsley, sea salt, pepper, cayenne, nutmeg, ketchup, and Worcestershire sauce in a large bowl. Knead with your hands until well mixed, then add the beaten egg and squish well until a little gluey. Form the mixture into a loaf shape with your hands.

Place the meatloaf in a roasting pan lined with parchment paper. Strew the canned crushed tomatoes and cherry tomatoes along the top and sprinkle with sea salt, pepper, and oregano. Bake until cooked through, about 1 hour.

Slice the meatloaf thickly and serve with green beans or watercress.

anchovy

Salt-cured anchovies in oil are a life-saver in the kitchen, injecting character and charm. Look for large, plump, fleshy anchovies from the Cantabrian sea of Spain (e.g. Ortiz) and put them to work on meats, vegetables, salads, and pizzas.

anchovy bruschetta Rub cut tomatoes over a split baguette, squeezing out the flesh and juices. Brush with garlicky olive oil, and broil until scorchy. Top with anchovy fillets and serve with drinks.

tapenade Purée $1\frac{1}{4}$ cups pitted black olives with $\frac{2}{3}$ cup drained tuna in oil, 4 anchovy fillets, 1 tbsp rinsed capers, a pinch of dried red pepper flakes, 1 tbsp each Dijon mustard and lemon juice, and pepper in a blender. Gradually blend in 3 tbsp extra virgin olive oil to make a paste. Serve on halved cherry tomatoes.

anchovy-chili butter Soften $\frac{2}{3}$ cup butter and fold in 10 minced anchovy fillets, 2 minced hot red chili peppers, and 1 crushed garlic clove. Serve with steak or steamed veggies.

anchovy-roast lamb Cut 16 slits in a leg of lamb. Push $\frac{1}{2}$ anchovy or a rosemary sprig into each, pour oil from the anchovy can over, and roast at 400°F until done to your liking.

anchoïade Pound 24 anchovy fillets with 2 tbsp tomato paste and 2 garlic cloves. Beat in $\frac{1}{4}$ cup extra virgin olive oil, 1 tbsp orange juice, and pepper. Spoon onto hard-boiled quail eggs.

anchovy, lemon & parmesan dressing Blend 2 crushed garlic cloves, 3 anchovy fillets, 1 tsp Dijon mustard, 1 tsp sugar, 1 tbsp lemon juice, 1 tbsp grated Parmesan, sea salt, and pepper until smooth. Slowly blend in 7 tbsp light olive oil. Drizzle over lettuce leaves.

lamb chop curry

SERVES 4

This spice mix is as close as I can get to a good, old-fashioned curry powder, the sort we loved before we started grinding our own spices.

$1/2$ cup plain yogurt

sea salt

8 well-trimmed lamb rib chops

1 onion, peeled

2 tbsp vegetable oil

1 tbsp grated fresh ginger

2 garlic cloves, crushed

1 tbsp tomato paste

$1^1/3$ cups peas (shelled fresh
  or frozen)

SPICE MIX

$1/4$ tsp each ground coriander,
  cumin, fenugreek, ginger,
  black pepper, cayenne,
  and turmeric

For the spice mix, combine all the spices in a bowl and stir well. Mix 1 tsp of this curry powder with the yogurt and 1 tsp sea salt. Toss the lamb chops in the spiced yogurt until lightly coated.

Halve and slice the onion. Heat the oil in a frying pan and cook the onion until soft, about 10 minutes. Add the ginger, garlic, and remaining curry powder, stirring. Add the lamb chops and their marinade, and brown lightly, turning once.

Add the tomato paste and $1^3/4$ cups water, and bring to a simmer. Cook gently, uncovered, until the lamb is tender and the sauce has thickened, 30 to 40 minutes.

Cook the peas in simmering, salted water for 5 minutes, then drain and add to the curry. Serve with rice.

chocolate

fruit

chocolate

fruit

rosy peaches with basil

Peaches are so perfect they need very little to make them extra special—just a quick poach in basil-scented rosé wine and a few adoring strawberries.

SERVES 4

4 unblemished, ripe peaches
$3/4$ cup sugar
10 basil leaves, plus extra
  for serving
$1^3/4$ cups rosé wine
1 small box strawberries

To peel the peaches, lightly score the skin from top to bottom and dunk them in a pan of simmering water for 10 seconds. Remove and peel under cold running water.

Combine the sugar, basil leaves, and rosé wine in a small saucepan, and bring to a boil, stirring. Tuck in the peaches and poach gently for 5 to 10 minutes, depending on ripeness. Gently remove the peaches.

Boil the liquid briskly until it is syrupy. Set aside to cool, then strain. Wash the strawberries but do not hull.

To serve, drizzle the rosé syrup over the peaches. Coat the strawberries in the syrup and arrange them next to the peaches. Scatter a few fresh basil leaves over.

chocolate honeycomb crêpes

Seductively dark chocolate crêpes are topped with crunchy honeycomb and yogurt. If you can't find confectionery honeycomb, crunch up a chocolate-coated honeycomb bar and scatter on top.

SERVES 4

²/₃ cup all-purpose flour
3¹/₂ tbsp cocoa powder, plus
   extra for dusting
3 tbsp honey
pinch of salt
2 large eggs
²/₃ cup milk
2 oz confectionery honeycomb
2 oz bittersweet chocolate
4 tsp butter
¹/₂ cup thick plain yogurt,
   chilled
1 tsp powdered sugar

To make the crêpe batter, blend the flour, cocoa powder, honey, salt, eggs, and milk in a food processor until smooth and creamy. Let the batter rest in the fridge for at least 30 minutes.

Roughly chop the honeycomb and set aside. Melt the chocolate in a heatproof bowl set over a pan of simmering water, and keep warm.

Melt 1 tsp butter in a crêpe pan or small nonstick frying pan over a medium heat. Add a ladleful of batter and swirl to cover the bottom thinly. Cook until set on top, 1 to 2 minutes, then turn and briefly cook the other side. Keep warm while you cook the remaining crêpes, adding 1 tsp butter to the pan each time.

Serve the crêpes on warm plates, folded, rolled, or loosely draped. Top with the yogurt and dust with cocoa powder sifted with the powdered sugar. Scatter the honeycomb over and drizzle on the melted chocolate.

chocolate cashew mousse

This is a Mexican take on everyone's favorite choccy mousse, combining chocolate with cashews, and infusing the chocolate with chili pepper for a tingling warmth that comes through the richness.

SERVES 4

4 oz bittersweet chocolate
$^1/_2$ tsp dried hot pepper flakes
$^1/_2$ tsp ground cinnamon
1 oz roasted salted cashews,
  plus 4 extra to finish
3 large eggs, separated
4 tbsp honey

Roughly chop the chocolate and place in a heatproof bowl set over a pan of simmering water. As soon as it starts to melt, add the pepper flakes and cinnamon. Take the pan off the heat and stir until smooth. Let cool for 10 minutes.

Work the cashews in a blender or food processor until finely ground. Beat the egg yolks and honey in a bowl until smooth. Stir in the chocolate and ground cashews until smooth.

Beat the egg whites in a clean bowl until they form soft peaks, then gently fold into the chocolate mixture.

Spoon into four small pots and chill for 2 hours. To serve, top each mousse with a whole salted cashew.

extra

chocolate infusions
Add something more exciting than vanilla when you melt chocolate for brownies, puddings, sauces, and frostings.

chili chocolate
Infuse 4 oz melted chocolate with 1 seeded and finely sliced small, hot red chili pepper.

ginger chocolate
Infuse 4 oz melted chocolate with 1 tbsp chopped preserved stem ginger.

sea salt & pepper chocolate
Infuse 4 oz melted chocolate with 1/2 tsp sea salt and 1/2 tsp ground black pepper.

mayan chocolate
Infuse 4 oz melted chocolate with 1/2 tsp ground cinnamon, 1/2 tsp ground allspice, and a good grating of nutmeg.

vienna plum cake

A gloriously old-fashioned mittel-European cake that brings back memories of Viennese coffeehouses. Serve warm for dessert, or cool and serve with coffee.

SERVES 6 TO 8

$3/4$ cup ($1^{1}/_{2}$ sticks) butter, softened, plus extra for pan
$3/4$ cup + 1 tbsp granulated sugar
4 large eggs
$1/2$ tsp pure vanilla extract
$1^{2}/_{3}$ cups all-purpose flour
1 tsp baking powder
pinch of salt
10 small plums (or apricots)
powdered sugar for dusting

Heat the oven to 350°F. Butter an 11- by 8-inch rectangular baking pan and line with parchment paper.

Cream the butter and granulated sugar together until pale. Add the eggs, one at a time, beating well after each addition. Stir in the vanilla extract.

Sift the flour, baking powder, and salt together over the mixture and fold in well, until combined. Spoon the batter into the baking pan.

Cut the plums around their circumference, twist apart, and remove the pits. Arrange the fruit, cut side up, in rows on top of the batter. Bake until a thin skewer inserted in the cake comes out clean, about 30 minutes.

Let cool slightly, or to room temperature. Dust with powdered sugar, then cut into squares and serve.

yogurt

Yogurt is the modern cook's cream; delicate, lush, delicious—and full of healthy bacteria. When these bacteria are added to milk, they break down the milk sugars, releasing lactic acid, which thickens the milk into yogurt and gives it its slightly sour taste. Choose thick, plain, low-fat yogurt, or look for Greek-style yogurt and goat's and sheep's milk yogurts in healthfood and wholefood stores.

black pepper yogurt Beat 1 tbsp vodka and 1 tbsp powdered sugar into $1^3/_4$ cups thick plain yogurt. Scatter cracked black pepper on top. Use as a dip for strawberries.

yogurt cheese Put 2 cups thick plain yogurt in a large square of doubled cheesecloth and hang overnight to drain. Serve spoonfuls of the resulting yogurt cheese drizzled with honey, or with ripe cherries.

mango raita Whisk 2 cups thick plain yogurt with 1 tbsp honey and 1 tbsp chopped mint. Mix with 1 diced mango and scatter 1 tbsp shredded coconut on top. Serve with cakes and desserts.

fruit fool Purée 1 cup raspberries with 1 tbsp powdered sugar. Layer 2 cups raspberries and $1^3/_4$ cups thick plain yogurt in 4 glasses, top with the berry purée, and serve with ladyfingers.

chocolate yogurt Melt 4 oz bittersweet chocolate in a bowl set over gently simmering water. Let cool for 10 minutes, then beat in $1^3/_4$ cups plain yogurt. Spoon this over 8 pears or peaches, poached in sugar syrup.

caramel yogurt Scatter 2 tbsp brown sugar over $1^1/_4$ cups thick plain yogurt and leave for 10 minutes to melt. Swirl the melted sugar through the yogurt, then serve with cakes, desserts, and poached fruits.

yogurt ice cream

Wow! Yogurt is fantastic frozen, transformed into an incredibly refreshing "ice-cream" that you can serve for dessert, scoop into ice cream cones, or sandwich between sesame snaps or wafers.

SERVES 4 TO 6

1 lb (2 cups) thick plain yogurt, preferably Greek-style

$1/2$ cup powdered sugar

OPTIONS

12 sesame snaps or ice cream wafers

2 tbsp good honey

$1/2$ cup toasted walnuts or pecans

Whisk the yogurt and powdered sugar together, then churn in an ice-cream machine, following the manufacturer's instructions. Or, freeze in a loaf pan or plastic container for 1 hour, removing and beating the mixture three times at 30–minute intervals to break up the ice crystals, then freeze until firm. Let soften for 15 to 30 minutes before serving.

Yogurt ice cream sandwiches: cut the ice cream into blocks the same size as the sesame snaps or wafers. Put each block between two snaps or wafers, then re-freeze on a tray until ready to serve.

Yogurt ice cream with honey and nuts: cut into thick slabs, drizzle with honey, and scatter toasted walnuts or pecans on top.

Soft-serve yogurt ice cream: remove from the freezer after 2 to 3 hours, when it is still all gloopy and soft. Serve in glasses with a drizzle of honey and a scattering of toasted walnuts or pecans.

cranberry blondies

White chocolate makes elegantly pale blondies instead of the usual brunette brownies, and cranberries give them that little touch of pink that blondes love to wear. Cut into small cubes for coffee, or larger squares for those emergency chocolate situations.

MAKES 25 SMALL,
OR 9 LARGE

$3/4$ cup + 2 tbsp ($1^3/4$ sticks) butter, plus extra for pan
10 oz good-quality white chocolate, chopped
3 large eggs
$1/2$ cup granulated sugar
$1/2$ tsp pure vanilla extract
$1^1/2$ cups all-purpose flour
pinch of salt
1 tbsp grated orange zest
$2/3$ cup dried cranberries
powdered sugar for dusting

Heat the oven to 350°F. Lightly butter an 11- by 7-inch rectangular baking pan and line the bottom with parchment paper.

In a heatproof bowl set over a pan of barely simmering water, melt the butter with 5 oz of the white chocolate, whisking well until smooth. Remove from the heat and let cool slightly.

In a separate bowl, beat the eggs, granulated sugar, and vanilla together until pale. Beat in the melted white chocolate mixture.

Fold in the flour and salt, then the remaining chopped chocolate, the orange zest, and three-fourths of the cranberries. Pour into the prepared pan and strew the rest of the cranberries on top. Bake until the top is firm and the inside is still a bit soft, about 20 minutes.

Let cool in the pan. Cut into small or large squares, then dust with powdered sugar and serve.

berry couscous

Couscous is the most elegant of comfort foods, especially when tossed with rose water and fresh berries that ping in the mouth. Serve with a sweet, creamy almond milk, for sipping or for pouring over the top.

SERVES 4

1²/₃ cups couscous
2 tbsp powdered sugar
1 tsp rose water or
   orange-flower water
1 cup blueberries
1 cup raspberries
2 tbsp pistachios, sliced
ALMOND MILK
1 cup ground almonds
¹/₂ tsp ground cinnamon
2 tbsp powdered sugar
2 cups milk

To make the almond milk, combine the ground almonds, cinnamon, sugar, and milk in a blender and blend until smooth. Strain through a fine sieve, then pour into a bottle and chill.

Place the couscous and sugar in a large heatproof bowl. Pour 2 cups boiling water over the top and stir through, then cover and leave until absorbed, about 30 minutes.

Break up the couscous and fluff it up a bit with your fingers. Add the rose water and berries, and lightly toss.

Divide the couscous among four small bowls and scatter the pistachios on top. Shake the bottle of almond milk until frothy, and pour into four small chilled glasses to accompany the couscous.

sticky lemon pudding

This self-saucing pudding is a great family favorite, forming a pillow of soft, golden, lemon sponge cake on top, with a tangy lemony sauce underneath.

SERVES 4

5 tbsp butter, plus extra for the baking dish
3/4 cup + 2 1/2 tbsp granulated sugar
2 tsp grated lemon zest
3 large eggs, separated
7 tbsp all-purpose flour, sifted
1 cup milk
7 tbsp lemon juice (around 3 lemons)
powdered sugar for dusting

Heat the oven to 350°F. In a food processor, beat the butter, granulated sugar, and lemon zest together until pale. Beat in the egg yolks, one at a time. Add the flour and milk alternately to make a smooth batter, beating well. Lastly, beat in the lemon juice.

In a large bowl, beat the egg whites until firm but not stiff, then fold the two mixtures together.

Pour into a buttered 4-cup baking dish and set in a baking pan. Half-fill the pan with hot water. Bake until the pudding is lightly browned and set on top, with a soft base of gooey lemon sauce, about 50 minutes.

Remove the dish from the water, dust the pudding with powdered sugar, and serve immediately.

good things to know

arborio rice A tough, plump superfino rice with a high starch content, grown in northern Italy. Use for risotto and rice puddings.

beancurd/tofu A bland white curd made from soybeans. Available fresh in soft (silken) and firmer varieties, and in long-life packages.

black beans Salted, fermented black soybeans, available vacuum-packed or in cans from Chinese markets. Throw a spoonful into stir-fries and noodle dishes.

buckwheat noodles/soba Dried buckwheat noodles available from Japanese markets and wholefood stores. Great for cold noodle salads.

bulghur wheat Steamed, dried, and cracked wheat kernels available from Middle Eastern markets and from wholefood stores.

capers The tiny green buds of a Mediterranean shrub. Buy packed in salt, and rinse before use. Available from large supermarkets.

cha plu A soft, tender green leaf (*piper sarmentosum*) used in Asian cooking. Sold in glossy, green bunches in Thai and Vietnamese markets.

chicken stock To make your own, rinse $4^{1}/_{2}$ lb chicken bones and cover with 4 quarts cold water. Bring to a boil, then simmer for 10 minutes, skimming off any froth. Add 2 finely sliced onions, 2 chopped carrots, 2 chopped celery stalks, and 2 finely chopped leeks, and simmer for 2 to 3 hours, skimming occasionally. Strain, discarding bones and vegetables, and let cool. Refrigerate overnight. Remove any fat that has risen to the surface, and freeze until needed.

chinese rice wine Made from glutinous rice and used rather like sherry in cooking, Chinese rice wine, or *shao hsing*, is available from Asian markets.

chocolate Choose the finest bittersweet or semisweet chocolate with a high percentage of chocolate liquor—at least 35%.

chorizo A highly flavored pork sausage, sold dried or fresh. Spanish chorizo is made with smoked pork, Mexican chorizo with fresh pork.

couscous Tiny pearls of semolina flour used in both savory and sweet dishes throughout the Middle East. Look for the pre-steamed, quick-cooking variety.

daikon A large, long, white radish with a refreshing flavor. Delicious freshly grated as a relish or slow-cooked in soups.

feta Salted fresh cheese sold in blocks in delicatessens, supermarkets, and Greek markets. Look for extra-creamy feta made from sheep's or goat's milk.

fish sauce A thin, salty sauce made from fermented fish and squid, used as a condiment in Thailand (nam pla) and Vietnam (nuoc mam).

harissa A spicy paste of dried red chili peppers and garlic. The best sort is available in jars from specialty markets. If buying in tubes, dilute with olive oil and taste for strength before using.

hoisin sauce A thick, sweet, pungent sauce made from fermented soybeans, sugar, vinegar, salt, garlic, chili, and sesame oil. A much nicer choice for pork or duck than the overly sweet plum sauce.

jalapeño peppers Keep a jar of pickled green jalapeño (pronounced hal-a-pen-yo) peppers in the fridge for those spontaneous taco moments. Available from major supermarkets.

jamon Fragrant cured ham, the Spanish equivalent of Italian prosciutto.

kaffir lime leaves Glossy leaves with a heavenly citrus smell. Fresh is best, available from Asian markets.

mirin A light, sweet Japanese rice wine used for sauces, dressings, and marinades. I love it in vinaigrettes as well. Available from Asian markets and most supermarkets.

mozzarella Fresh mozzarella comes in smooth, milky-white balls known as "bocconcini," packed in their own whey. It is infinitely superior to mass-produced mozzarella. Delicate buffalo mozzarella, made from buffalo milk, is ruinously good.

olives Pay extra for good French, Greek, Spanish, or Italian olives, and don't worry about pitting them. Avoid those awful pre-pitted, dyed-black olives that appear on cheap pizzas.

paprika My favorite is Spanish smoked paprika, with its rich smoky flavor and good heat levels.

pink peppercorns The small, dried red berries of the Brazilian pepper tree, with an aromatic peppery flavor. And yes, I only use them because they are pretty.

preserved lemons Whole lemons preserved in a salty brine, available from Middle Eastern markets and major supermarkets. Rinse well, and use the rind only.

rice noodles Dried, flat, white, semi-transparent rice-flour noodles, also known as rice stick noodles. Available in various widths.

rice vermicelli Dried, brittle, semi-transparent noodles (thinner than rice noodles) made from extruded rice-flour paste. These noodles turn white when cooked.

rice wine vinegar A clear, mild vinegar made from fermented rice, from Asian markets. Fabulous with sliced cucumber and in salad dressings.

rose water A clear, light distillation of rose petals. Available from Middle Eastern markets and major supermarkets.

saffron The orange-red stigmas of the crocus plant. Expensive, but worth investing in and using sparingly. Crush with a tiny amount of water before adding to your cooking.

sea salt Upgrade to delicate sea salt flakes (e.g. Maldon) for table use. It makes all the difference in the world.

sesame oil A dark, aromatic oil made from toasted sesame seeds, to be used sparingly in Asian food and in vinaigrettes.

shiitake mushrooms Dried black mushrooms that add rich, earthy flavor and a meaty texture to Asian dishes. To reconstitute, cover with boiling water and let soak for at least 30 minutes before draining. If using the soaking water, strain out any grit first.

sugar Seek out natural unrefined sugars, for more flavor and health benefits.

tahini A thick, creamy, nutty paste made from husked and ground white sesame seeds. Available in jars from Middle Eastern markets and wholefood stores.

tamarind concentrate A sour-tasting fruit sold as a pulp or, more conveniently, a refined concentrate in small jars, available from supermarkets.

tobiko Very fine, crunchy Japanese fish roe, often colored red, salmon orange, or wasabi green. Available frozen from Japanese markets.

togarashi A popular Japanese condiment made of dried chili pepper, sansho pepper, sesame seeds, and seaweed. Available from Japanese markets.

tomato paste A concentrated tomato paste sold in small tubes, jars, and cans.

tortillas Flat, unleavened pancakes made from cornmeal or wheat flour. Available from supermarkets.

vanilla extract Pure vanilla extract is pricey, but so aromatic that you need use only a few drops. Avoid cheap vanilla flavoring, which is artificially flavored.

vegetable stock I recommend Marigold Swiss Vegetable Bouillon Powder with its fresh, carroty taste. To make your own stock, heat 2 tbsp olive oil in a large pot. Add 2 finely sliced onions and 2 each finely chopped carrots, celery stalks, and tomatoes. Cook for 5 minutes, stirring. Add 5 cups boiling water and simmer for 30 minutes. Strain, cool, and freeze until needed.

wasabi A green, pungent root, known as Japanese horseradish. Devilishly hot, available in a powder form (dilute with water to taste) or in tubes.

metric equivalents

oven temperatures

Fahrenheit	Celsius	Oven level
275°F	140°C	Very low
300°F	150°C	Low
325°F	170°C	Low
350°F	180°C	Moderate
375°F	190°C	Moderate
400°F	200°C	Hot
425°F	220°C	Hot
450°F	230°C	Very hot

weight

$1/4$ oz	7.5 g
$1/2$ oz	15 g
$3/4$ oz	20 g
1 oz	30 g
$1 1/2$ oz	40 g
2 oz	55 g
$2 1/2$ oz	75 g
3 oz	85 g
$3 1/2$ oz	100 g
4 oz	115 g
$4 1/2$ oz	125 g
5 oz	140 g
6 oz	170 g
7 oz	200 g
8 oz	225 g
9 oz	255 g
10 oz	285 g
11 oz	310 g
12 oz	340 g
13 oz	370 g
14 oz	400 g
15 oz	425 g
1 lb	450 g
1 lb 2 oz	500 g
$1 1/4$ lb	600 g
$1 1/2$ lb	700 g
1 lb 10 oz	750 g
$1 3/4$ lb	800 g
2 lb	900 g
$2 1/4$ lb	1 kg

length

$1/4$ inch	5 mm
$1/2$ inch	1 cm
1 inch	2.5 cm
2 inches	5 cm
3 inches	7.5 cm
4 inches	10 cm
5 inches	12 cm
6 inches	15 cm
7 inches	18 cm
8 inches	20 cm
9 inches	23 cm
10 inches	25 cm
11 inches	28 cm
12 inches	30 cm

index

acknowledgments
The publishers wish to thank the following companies for the loan of props for photography:
Designers Guild, King's Road, London SW3;
Divertimenti, 33/4 Marylebone High Street, London W1;
Skandium, 86 Marylebone High Street, London W1.